Pembrokeshire Standing Stones

Jill Young

The images used in this book were scanned from the originals by the Royal Commission on the Ancient and Historical Monuments of Wales. With the exceptions of the first and last, the paintings have been set out alphabetically by parish. Each image is identified with a number that relates to the map on page 34, the National Grid Reference (NGR) of the location and the National Principal Record Number (NPRN) of the site in the National Monuments Record for Wales. The scanned images and further information and records about each stone can be found online at www.coflein.gov.uk either by browsing Pembrokeshire standing stones or by searching for the individual NPRN.

ISBN: 978–1-84527-453-5

Cover design: Eleri Owen
Location map of Pembrokeshire: Alison Davies

Photographs are from the National Monuments Record of Wales:
J. C. Young Pembrokeshire Standing Stones Paintings Collection

First published in 2015
Gwasg Carreg Gwalch, Llanrwst
☏ 01758 750432 🖷 01758 750438
books@carreg-gwalch.com
Website: www.carreg-gwalch.com

In memory of my late husband Peter
who gave me support in every way
and helped me to find the stones;
and to thank our children Rory and Katrina
who did so much to encourage me
and to bring the project to fruition.

Contents

Foreword

The paintings in this book convey a passion for the great stones that prehistoric peoples set in place across the land we now call Pembrokeshire. Jill Young was fascinated by these monuments. She trudged through fields and across moors to find and study them. The dense, compelling paintings that she made as a result express facts of shape, tone and texture and, more than this, invoke the personality and presence of these stones, which stand like ancient sentinels to a deep past, witnesses to thousand upon thousand seasons.

The Welsh *maen hir,* 'long stone', has been transmitted through Breton to the French term *menhir* known internationally by archaeologists. Long, vertically placed stones can be found across the globe, but they are particularly characteristic of Atlantic Europe and especially Wales and western Britain, Ireland and Brittany: Pembrokeshire is a rich hunting ground for them. Here, most were probably put up by Early Bronze Age people, between around 2500 and 1400 BC, though some may be even older. We will never understand the subtleties of the meanings they held for farmers and hunters four millennia ago but it is likely that there were varied reasons why communities invested so much time and care to source vast stones and stand them tall and prominent. Certainly, some were parts of processional routes or ritual henges and alignments now lost from view. Some marked burials; others probably signified boundaries between territories or were way-makers to guide travellers.

Jill Young began her hunt for menhirs in 1981, shortly after she had retired with her husband Peter to the slate quarry settlement of Abereiddy, where they had long had connections. Jill set herself the task to visit every standing stone listed in 1966 by the Royal Commission on the Ancient and Historical Monuments of Wales, make notes of what was known about them and record each stone accurately in paint. All the images matched in medium and size – oil paintings 5 inches by 8 – and were utterly consistent in style. She finished the whole set in 1984, when she and Peter began their loving restoration of a Georgian sea-captain's house and gardens across the Teifi sands from Pembrokeshire: Bryn-y-mor.

Jill had studied at Wimbledon School of Art and the University of London and taught art in London and Gloucestershire. She largely resisted the shockwaves of twentieth-century art and looked back to Dutch masters of still life and British landscape painters of the Romantic era. Her paintings of the Pembrokeshire stones seem out of their time – their faithfulness is reminiscent of topographical artists in the eighteenth century (entirely fitting in a project to record remains authoritatively) while her fascination with restless trees, full moons, heavy skies and lightning conjures feelings of timelessness and awe just as Romantic-era artists sought to do. But Modernist influences from her formative years are also present, in the mood of uneasy drama that recalls the paintings Paul Nash and John Piper made of megaliths, and in the sense that these stones 'own' their landscapes just as Henry Moore's giant bronze kings and queens hold dominion over parks and hills.

The 53 paintings in this book form a remarkable sequence by an artist striving to say something more than can be said one painting at a time – seeking to take on a subject systematically, like the Buck brothers engraving Britain's castles in the eighteenth century or Monet painting his lily pond in every light and season. Although other menhirs have been found in Pembrokeshire, all the famous ones are represented here, and the combined effect is inspirational.

As Secretary of the Royal Commission in 2011, I was delighted that through Jill's generosity we were able to add scans of all these paintings to our online archive, Coflein, where they can be found alongside other information about each stone. Shortly afterwards the entire collection of originals was secured permanently by the National Library of Wales.

Sadly, Jill Young could not see this book through the press before she died. But now completed by her children, Rory and Katrina, with Gwasg Garreg Gwalch, it is both a celebration of beguiling monuments and an eloquent memorial to a talented artist and writer.

Dr Peter Wakelin

Known unto God are all his Works from the beginning of the World.
ACTS 15, verse 18

Painting the Stones

The beginning of the work was the painting of eight rubbing stones on Manor Farm, Llanrhian, where each one had its own lovely landscape and character in spite of being erected only in the last century. Then the idea developed into discovering and recording every authenticated ancient standing stone in the county of Pembrokeshire.

The work itself proved to be truly gargantuan because of the number of stones. It was not sufficient to paint and photograph them; drawings had to be made of all sides, compass directions taken and history uncovered, leading to much research.

The owners of the land on which the stones stand, the Keepers of the Stones as they shall be called, were most kind in allowing access to their property. Great care was always taken to find them, and this sometimes led to long searches, and interesting meetings and conversations.

In many cases it seemed as if the stones were determined to hide themselves; they could be seen from a distance yet disappeared when approached. Alternatively they went out of their way to make themselves so obvious they were almost missed in their manner.

The *meini hirion*, even those which have been broken and are pathetic remnants of the grand sculptures they once were, fill the area in which they stand with an atmosphere that can be startlingly strong at the first encounter. Their influence increased as work proceeded until the painting became like a portrait of a person.

Much wonderful landscape was seen, but as habitation has encroached on the wild country through the centuries, standing stones are to be found in unexpected sites. They have been lost by being incorporated into buildings. Some stand beside main roads for all to see, others have been built into field hedges or used as gate posts, hide in gardens or stand sentinel on wild hillsides. The majority are on farm land cultivated since the Enclosures, where they are generally cared for and respected.

Despite the use of Ordnance Survey maps, finding the stones was an adventure and the sudden sight of a stone was nearly always a dramatic experience; we felt we were almost intruding on their privacy and they were watching our movements. It would be interesting to observe whether these sensations differ with the seasons of the year, cycles of the moon etc., but with such a large project it has been impossible to revisit the stones with any frequency.

Some sites are disappointing pictorially: problems of obscured distances and high hedges running horizontally across the middle of the picture present difficulty in arranging a composition while painting the stone as large as possible in its own setting. Therefore in one or two cases it has been necessary to 'see through' to the landscape beyond. However, usually it is an impressive experience. To see a monolith standing in the landscape is like coming upon a sculpture by Henry Moore in a natural setting. As shapes alone they are nearly all marvellous in one way or another but when they are moved to museums, as some stones have been, their impact is negligible.

A perfect landscape could not be *chosen* to paint behind the stones. Very often the light which described the shape best was not right for the most beautiful or significant scenery. However, the Pembrokeshire countryside has a particular beauty and magic of its own anywhere, when it is not spoiled by ugly modern building.

Many *meini hirion* are covered in lichens varying in colour from the darkest browns, black, grey/greens to brilliant cadmium yellow and orange; occasionally rust/red ones appear. Birds rest in flight on the pointed tops and their white droppings emphasise the curves of the stones. The lower parts of many are polished to a wonderful patina by the rubbing of livestock against them. Frequently they stand in small hollows where water collects in the sheep-puddled soil. Perhaps this is the reason why the grass grows so brilliantly green around their bases in spite of being closely grazed; some might say it is energy emanating from them that produces luxuriant growth even in rough mountain pasture. Dowsers have found that water lines cross below standing stones.

It is certain that they have a particular attraction for animals as can be seen from the tracks leading to and from them; the dowser's track lines? While painting a *maen hir* among quietly grazing sheep a ewe seen making directly for the stone has stopped dead at the sight of an intruder. Mountain ponies have swerved off course for the same reason; in fact some farmers observe that livestock choose to give birth to their young near stones or tumuli. This could of course be their need to seek shelter but also perhaps for the same reasons that humans have chosen to visit them.

As this study proceeded it became obvious that there were many similarities in the shapes of monoliths. Sometimes these were immediately apparent but usually it was not until the drawings and paintings were started on site that the likenesses were noticed. When any objective reproduction is undertaken, the eye first sums up the general size, shape, colour, texture, tone and form of the subject whether it is human or inanimate. With this established in the mind the general shape of the subject is drawn; it was at this stage the similarities became apparent in the curves, straight lines, notches, depressions and bulges. Except in the case of stones which have obviously been badly broken, it seems there must have been some intended similarity. Cynics will say that this idea is fanciful as they are just weathered rough quarried stones, or boulders rolled along by glaciers. It should however be remembered that these monoliths were of immense significance, whether this was religious, meteorological or tribal, and therefore would have been shaped and sited in no haphazard fashion.

In so many cases, irrespective of weathering and regardless of slim or massive proportion, the tops are pointed, domed or chisel-shaped. Frequently there seems to be a front, and a back which is more or less flat, but with different angles to the silhouette. In front, the top drops down to a flattish face which ends at a ledge or bulge. This then continues downwards, sometimes curving out in a belly-like protuberance, to end either in another ledge or an undercut angle. Another straightish face then descends to ground level. Frequently there are signs of notches in the tops, and vertical facets at the sides.

Some stones are obviously four-sided, while others are basically triangular even though they may have five actual sides at ground level. The slim pillars of pairs come into the latter category. Several others are fundamentally four-sided, but the 'front' is angled to form a 'nose'.

The most obvious similarities within the different categories can be seen in the contrasting so-called male and female shapes of pairs.

Indented marks have been noticed, varying from roughly one-inch-deep circular holes which could be the remains of cup marks or something similar, occasionally in pairs, to the spectacular twisted shapes on the Puncheston village and Dolau Maen stones. There is a series of holes and vertical grooves on one of the stones at Cilgwyn Farm, and the beautiful stone at St Catherine's, Haroldston West has many vertical V-shaped grooves. The stone near Pen Parke has two curved vertical ridges on one side. As the stones have been standing for thousands of years any marks will have been softened by constant weathering, but many do seem to have been made on purpose. Since actual human representational carvings have now been dated to the Neolithic Period there is surely no need to dismiss all these marks and the shapes of the stones, as having been caused by weathering or accident.

The Fate of Monoliths

The fate of megalithic monuments has varied through the centuries. In early Christian times they were allowed to remain, churches were built on pagan sites, stone circles incorporated into churchyard walls, and standing stones 'Christianised' by Baptism and the carving of crosses and Christian symbols upon them. The Fathers of the early Church were wise in not destroying the ancient sites when they introduced the New Faith.

At the time of the Reformation many Christian holy places, including wells, were destroyed, though the veneration of them would have been likely to emanate from the pre-Christian period. At Llanfair Nantgwyn, 'Pistyll Meigan', a place of pilgrimage, was destroyed. Local dignitaries received orders from 'Her Magestie's Privy Council to pull down and utterlie deface all reliques and monuments of that chappell not leaving one stone uppon another'.

In the post-Reformation period of the Commonwealth the destruction began in earnest and the iconclasts set out to remove as many traces as possible of any graven images, whether they were Christian art or the pre-Christian structures which they did not understand. Wonderful fresco paintings were destroyed when plaster was chipped off or white-washed, stone carvings defaced or destroyed by the ton, marvellous glass smashed to atoms and parish churches and cathedrals desecrated. Megalithic monuments suffered in a similar manner when cromlechau and standing stones were overthrown.

In 1648, the year before the Commonwealth, John Aubrey discovered the enormous megaliths at

Avebury. These and Stonehenge were then relatively unnoticed until the early years of the eighteenth century and the increase of land cultivation on a large scale, when William Stukely, doctor and clergyman, began a series of plans and drawings to record both sites. During the years he was engaged in this work local men were systematically destroying the majority of the Avebury stones by uprooting them with levers and splitting them with fire, water and hammers. The man, Thomas Robinson, who engineered the destruction, was labelled Stone Killer by Stukely, who in his book *Avebury*, published a portrait of him in front of the graphic representation of stones being cracked by fire. This was not done without risk; the finding of the skeleton of the Barber surgeon beneath one of the monoliths he was helping to destroy is proof enough.

At the time of the Enclosures many more monoliths must have been destroyed, where they impeded ploughing because they happened to be in the 'wrong' place. Likewise tumuli were ploughed over and cromlechau cracked up for building stone. Further destruction occurred in the late eighteenth and early nineteenth centuries when men like Richard Fenton developed an enthusiasm for antiquities and started opening tumuli and scattering their contents in search of treasure.

Similarly they dug under standing stones, causing them to fall, and seemed disappointed when all that was found were bits of bone and crude pottery. Criticism must not be too severe as they were not always the first on the scene; people have robbed graves for many centuries the world over in search of treasure, despite legends of spirits which guard ancient places and the curses they put on those who meddle with them.

Indeed much gratitude should be felt towards these early antiquarians for the untiring manner in which they travelled through difficult country, devoting time, energy and their own money to documenting objects of historic interest.

At this time painters such as Constable, Turner, Girtin and others were influenced by the interest shown in megaliths by earlier artists, and captured in their paintings the romantic atmosphere of such places. The tradition continues to the present day as the great contemporary artists John Piper and Henry Moore have drawn and painted Megalithic monuments.

In spite of this, many sites they recorded have been destroyed and are still disappearing. No doubt stones still lie hidden in hedges, or in the bottom of quarries, where they may yet be found and recognised, but unless they can be re-erected in their exact positions on their original sites their value is gone.

Excavations of standing stones have largely left unanswered the questions of what kind of people set them up, how they did it, and for what purpose. Some scholars suggest that Neolithic people were conversant with a method of lightening the weight of huge rocks in order to make them float through the air, or were even able to precipitate them. Many legends tell of saints and giants hurling stones great distances. All this could be associated with the phenomenon of human levitation which has been known for centuries, but not understood; many records of it appear in the lives of saints, and it has been known to happen in recent times. It was said that S. Theresa of Avila, a sixteenth century nun and mystic, disciplined in mental prayer and contemplation, levitated frequently and on occasion had to be held down by her nuns.

A great sensation was caused in recent years when Professor A. Thom published his findings on the geometrical construction of stone circles. In his expert and detailed surveys he suggested that they were set out with the greatest accuracy. He concluded that to do this so-called primitive people must have been conversant with practical geometry, in order to set out elaborate designs and ellipses based on 'Pythagorean' triangles, a thousand years before the earliest mathematicians of classical Greece.

He found from inside the circles, or ellipses as they often proved to be, outlying stones could be sighted on alignments to hill-top sites which marked rising or setting points of the sun and moon at equinoxes. During the year, movements of major stars as well as the sun and moon could have been calculated from the centre of circles. His book, *Megalithic Sites in Britain*, published in 1967, proved highly controversial as most new ideas do; it also gave leads in fresh directions to the many people who are now working on different lines to discover the secrets of stones.

The stones which survive today are only the minutest remnant of thousands which once patterned the landscape. As so many have obviously been removed in past centuries, the single remaining ones are all the more precious, but it is harder to visualise their purpose. They could be outlying markers, or solitary members or circles or alignments, all that is left of great and powerful geometric shapes. It is surely essential that their purpose should be better understood before yet others are disturbed in any way. Those that have been moved, even to re-erect them when fallen, have been found to have become different in character from those remaining in their original positions.

There is no doubt stones have been moved great distances as in the case of Stonehenge where the blue stones of the inner circle are 'foreign'. The nearest place to the locality from where they could have come is Pembrokeshire. Though some people have disputed this idea and declared they were moved to Salisbury Plain by glaciers, no other stones of the same type have been found in the area except those used in a long barrow in Wiltshire. (Geoffrey of Monmouth, although his historical facts are dismissed, said that the stones were not found at Stonehenge, but were brought by Merlin from Ireland where they stood as a Temple.)

Similarly, it is thought stones were moved about in Pembrokeshire, though it is there more likely that they were deposited by glaciers; yet, considering the recognised movement of rocks to Stonehenge, it is possible they were intentionally moved long distances within the county. In this study the temptation to chip for samples for identification has been resisted but it is known many standing stones are composed of spotted dolorite, the blue stone of Preseli.

It has always been supposed that this area was one of particular holiness to Neolithic man because of the number of remaining edifices. It is true that the whole of the west coast of Britain is richly endowed with standing stones and other monuments, from Cornwall to Scotland, with a very large number of sties in the Hebrides.

Another suggestion is that barrows act as power

collectors and standing stones as lightning conductors in some way, balancing thunderstorm activity over the British Isles. Maps showing distribution of thunderstorms give evidence of more occurring on the East of Britain but with less ferocity than those on the West, where there are more megalithic sites. It is certain that in Pembrokeshire they are extremely dramatic when they do occur. Legends tell of violent thunderstorms breaking over the heads of people disturbing ancient sites; it has also been recorded that the same thing has been experienced in recent times. On many occasions when visiting and painting stones, though they were not being tampered with, thunder rolled round the sky ominously, but fortunately lightning did not strike.

Ley Lines

The aim in the carrying out of this study has been to incorporate all theories and hypotheses which include standing stones. Although some are perhaps far-fetched, most, like folk memories, contain some virtue; old sayings disparaged by scientific Victorians are now found to contain more than a little truth.

Ley lines may be laughed at, but the theory should at least be examined for any clue that would help our uncertainty. It is a basic scientific premise that when studying anything, the most important asset is an open mind.

In 1921, a Herefordshire corn merchant, antiquarian and amateur photographer called Alfred Watkins reined in his horse to look at the view from the Bredwardine Hills. At that moment he experienced the revelation of a secret which had been hidden for thousands of years. He saw a vision of Neolithic Britain with a network of glowing lines running perfectly straight across the country. They linked ancient places of sanctity such as standing stones, burial mounds, wells, fords, moats, castles, and churches built on ancient sites. He called these Ley Lines, and spent the rest of his life confirming his discovery, writing, lecturing, researching and exciting a storm of criticism from traditional antiquarians. In spite of this no one has been able to DISprove his theories and many have benefited in interest and enjoyment from them.

Watkins believed ley lines were tracks used by early man; in later years researchers have felt that, though this may be true, leys could also follow invisible lines of power running across the countryside; certain points such as standing stones, mounds, circles etc. may be energy accumulations from where power can be taken or absorbed, or are like relays for further transmission of energy. It has been suggested that these lines of power traverse the whole world; that they mark the pattern of places where the earth's force could be tapped by those who knew how to use it for the benefit of plants, animals, and all mankind.

The Australian aborigines' Lines of Songs are believed by them to be the paths of their gods, and to traverse the continent.

Aerial photography has revealed mysterious visible straight lines in various parts of the world. Stretching across the Peruvian desert near Nazca is a network of lines imprinted in the subsoil beneath the eroded pampas. They are so straight they could have been made with a ruler. Intersecting them are other straight lines, and amongst them bird, plant and animal images.

In Bolivia even longer dead straight lines have been discovered, linking ancient places of sanctity and also Christian churches. The lines are kept open through the vegetation by the regular procession of Indian villagers along them.

Comparable straight lines can be picked up in Britain by joining hedgerows and parts of old tracks, earth banks, ancient monuments and stones, but as these islands have been so heavily populated and cultivated through the centuries the lines have been destroyed in most places. Everyone is familiar with the straight so-called Roman Roads; now many people believe these existed centuries before the Romans came to Britain.

Dowsing

The ancient art of dowsing is usually associated with finding water though it can be used for the divining of many things. Today it is common enough to see someone dowsing by mechanical means, searching beaches for coins with a metal detector, or water board staff looking for pipes or leaks underground.

In recent years, traditional dowsing has become a complete science in its own right. Many highly intelligent, sane practitioners have turned their attention to other fields of interest, including archaeology. Here their skills can be of the greatest help to archaeologists in discovering the most profitable sites in which to dig. They are able to pinpoint places in the field where various things, not only metal, can be found. This is valuable in saving time and objects from destruction when machines remove the top soil layer. The Gogmagog Hill figures in Cambridgeshire were discovered by dowsing and afterwards excavated.

Additionally, skilful dowsers are able to date items in time by using techniques similar to those for finding the depths of streams below ground. Their conclusions have been proved correct by modern methods of radiocarbon dating. T. C. Lethbridge dated Stonehenge accurately before radiocarbon testing was re-calibrated in 1968.

In 1969 a book called *The Pattern of the Past* by Guy Underwood was published. In it he observed that water lines, the apparent courses of streams, are inclined to meet and encircle Neolithic sites such as standing stones and barrows (or burial chambers). He discovered two other types of primary lines: track lines, the tracks animals naturally follow, terrestrial signal lines; and lines that are not water but similar to it, which he called aquastats.

These classes of line form patterns which dowsers can find round and under ancient sites. In the case of standing stones, water lines and aquastats will take spiral courses towards them. Churches, which are not always orientated as is popularly supposed, frequently have aquastats or water lines running up the nave. These end beneath the altar in a 'blind spring': the name for a centre where primary lines join and spread out. Underwood concluded that early architects knew about these patterns and that all religious structures from Neolithic times until the Renaissance were deliberately constructed with them in mind.

Sometimes a pendulum reacts at standing stone sites for no apparent reason. This is called by dowser Tom Graves a 'charge' because of its resemblance to an electrostatic charge. Either positive or negative reactions are given by these, and they change from time to time. When dowsing at the Rollright Circle he found charges altered as he went from stone to stone. He discovered a flow of power which seemed to travel above ground, nearly always in straight lines, from stone to stone around circles, thus forming a spin or rotation of power. These lines of charge shot off from the Rollright Circle at two different points for a considerable distance in dead straight lines a few feet wide. They may have a connection with Alfred Watkins' ley lines. Where these flow lines meet they form what Graves calls nodes. Structures sited on nodes he likens to acupuncture needles inserted into the Earth's body. He has found that even when one of these structures (or stones) has been moved (he quotes a certain mark stone) it still communicates with its original site.

This must mean that where pairs of standing stones have lost one partner, not only should it be possible for a competent dowser to find the site where the stone stood, but to track down the missing one: a very exciting prospect.

Concentrations of charge can be found on some sites, particularly standing stones, taking the form of a spiral release of energy which can be tapped at different heights on the stone. There are usually seven such tapping points, but smaller stones may only have the first five. The first point is below ground, the second just below ground level and the third just above ground. These three have no direct effect on the dowser but may be connected with the patterns discovered by Guy Underwood. The next point up is the overground stone to stone transmission height. Number five point affects the balance so that the dowser feels as if he is falling or being pushed to one side or the other. This changes with the lunar cycle. The next point, number six, acts in long distance overground transmissions. Number seven affects the spine muscles, produces a sensation of an electric shock and can throw the dowser backwards from the stone.

It seems there could be an interchange between the overground flow of power, and underground aquastats and water lines, and track lines.

Unsuspecting lay people have quite unknowingly touched stones and received the electric shock or falling sensations. Presumably this accounts for the name Tingle Stone in Gloucestershire and may be due to the presence of quartz.

Some dowsers experience a halo-like aura surrounding standing stones; it is not unusual for the sensitive to see an aura round people or objects; this might be similar to the lights mentioned in fairy stories and folk lore. The use of a halo of light is not confined to paintings by Christian artists and was frequently used by the Romans among other people, in paintings in fresco, and mosaics.

Dowsing is used in various forms of healing, one of the most important of which is Radionics. The basis of this therapy is the belief that all forms of life are incorporated within the electromagnetic energy field of the earth, and that each form has its own electromagnetic field. If there is interference in its pattern, illness or disease will result.

An intuitive, trained practitioner can dowse, with a series of mentally-posed questions by a process which is outside ordinary thinking, to discover the cause of disease in living organisms. The organic sample of the 'patient' and the remedy are put into the sample well of a radionic instrument which the practitioner uses as a channel through which to treat the living organism, whether it is human, animal or plant. Though this method of healing appears extraordinary it is in many cases more effective than conventional medicine.

Psychometry is another form of dowsing in which people with certain gifts are able to receive an impression or mental picture of objects with which they are in contact. By using this art practical psychometrists can help to discover facts about the riddle of standing stones. Many people are sceptical about such ideas, but animals are thought to have these sensitivities and many stories are told of their awareness of the supernatural. Perhaps, with man's progression through the centuries his sense of spirituality has been blinded by materialism. Neolithic people may have had senses which hardly exist in humans now.

'Gates'

While searching for standing stones the word gate, *yet, iet* appeared so frequently that it assumed more significance than the relatively modern meaning of barrier. They could be pairs of stones which were already conveniently set when the fields were laid out, or rather that the fields were positioned so the posts could be utilised to hang gates upon. Old traditions die hard, and if a pair of stones had been revered in the past there would be good reason for dressing them neatly and drilling them to take hooks and leaving them in situ. Two of the large stones in the alignment at Trellwyn Fawr Farm, Llanllawer have been drilled and a gate hung between them. Many gateways have been widened and the stones removed. Since the last war farm machinery has become too large to pass through the narrow gaps which horse-drawn carts could negotiate.

Guy Underwood attached the greatest importance to the part played in the earth's patterns by all ancient stones, whether they were monoliths, cromlechau, basin stones, rocking stones, sloping stones called Rostra, stone seats, heel stones, node stones (large stones at ground level in old walls), stone rows, parted stones, slab fences, bridges, spirit holes (small gaps covered with lintels in moorland walls) or stone gate posts. He identified all these on prehistoric sites as marking important places in the geodetic pattern of the earth. He thought some old gate posts were unnecessarily large for holding gates unless there had been some previous use and significance to them. In his dowsing work he discovered that many ancient stone posts marked important processional lines connecting ancient sites with each other, such as stone circles, mazes, monoliths etc.

This might link up with the findings and work done by Tom Graves at the broken hedge bank at Gors Fawr, and just shows how strong these unknown currents of power can be. This is discussed in the description of Gors Fawr standing stones and circle.

It seems they were indeed gates, not closed barriers as we know them, but openings, or as Alfred Watkins came to believe, the road itself. The modern meaning for the word gate appears to be a corruption of the original, which in most languages was a passage, a pass, or way through; perhaps in some places to eternity or timelessness.

Stones have been called Entrances to Fairyland. These small fairy creatures played a very real part in the beliefs of country people until a short time ago, and do perhaps even today. In some places they were thought to be the spirits of the dead. They traversed their special paths over land, water or even through walls, and it was considered very unlucky to get in their way or stop them. The paths were regarded by an Irish seer as arteries through which the magnetic current of the earth circulates.

Quartz

Many *meini hirion* are composed of conglomerates known as pudding stone. Folk lore tells us that these stones grew and multiplied. The belief that they actually grew in the ground was widespread, and was mentioned by a farmer in jest during the painting of the stones.

Some conglomerates contain a high proportion of quartz, a substance found frequently in varying quantities in standing stones. It is one of the elements most common in rocks and if subjected to intense pressure or vibration it becomes electrically charged. It has become the essential basic material in a great variety of electronic equipment. With its re-introduction and increasing use we may be on the verge of discovering secrets known to our distant ancestors, as some people think these properties may be connected with the hidden power of ley lines.

There must have been a good reason for taking stones containing quartz long distances to erect them as circles or single pillars. One only has to look at the crystals of the Tŷ Newydd Grug stone to appreciate this, and feel it was not put there just because it looked beautiful.

Composed of granite with seams of quartz, Le Grand Menhir Brise near Carnac, which was estimated to weigh 340 tons and stand 70 ft high before it fell, was taken at least fifty miles to the place where it stood on the coast of Brittany.

Quarts pebbles and fragments have been found with cremated burials, and offerings of quartz were made at holy wells. It was said that the Archdruid wore a ball of crystal which shone or became dull. Water was poured over quartz crystals and given as medicine to humans and animals. They were also used as charms, some of which were recorded as having been burnt in a lime kiln by a dissenting minister.

Some people consider that the very tip of the Great Pyramid consisted of gold with a crystal or diamond on the top, to draw force out of the ether.

Recently placed 'offerings' of small pieces of quartz were seen around the base of a high standing stone in Pembrokeshire in 1982.

However, it must be said that generally standing stones are composed of local stone, though all are thought to contain quartz in some form or another. Its presence is the suggested cause of fogging on some people's photographs of standing stones.

The Siting of Monoliths

When looking at a standing stone the observer may wonder why it is in that particular situation, whether it is on a bleak hillside or a rushy water-logged moor. They are rarely found on summits. In Pembrokeshire there are usually hills on the horizon and water is never far away. The tops of hills are often crowned by ancient structures, cairns, tumuli, hill forts, natural outcrops or notches in the silhouettes. An Ordnance Survey map will usually show a cromlech, burial mound or ancient track somewhere in the vicinity of the stone, or if these have gone, their names may survive in field or farm names. The idea then develops that once there were alignments of stones stretching out towards the horizon in the way that electricity pylons do today. Possibly Neolithic people just came upon a place to live and erect their stones. However, some scholars think that the British countryside was laid out purposely in a definite pattern, and Alfred Watkins was one of the first modern thinkers to conceive this idea.

Since the last War, Watkins' ideas have been reconsidered and developed by others who believe that China may hold the secret of Britain's early landscape planning. Before the advent of the Communist Regime in China, and still now to a lesser extent, great importance was given to the siting of new buildings. A geomancer, an expert in the ancient science of Feng Shui, would advise on the suitability of the location, and the effect of the new structure on the landscape whether it was a stone, tomb, or even a tree. The geomancer was able to detect the invisible magnetic forces which were believed to flow over the surface of the earth: the so-called dragon current which is composed of Male and Female elements. The female, Yin, negative, was symbolised by a white tiger and followed the low hills; the male Yang, positive, the blue dragon, ran along high hills and mountains. Where the two flows met were the best places, particularly where the current was most active at the meeting point of a mountain range and a line of low hills. In places like this they sited their tombs, as great importance was given to the belief that the forces acting upon the bodies of ancestors affected the destiny of their descendants. Consideration was also given to the scenery; ideally the tomb faced south with a hill behind it, and lower beautiful country in front. The current was scattered in wide open spaces, particularly when there were straight lines such as roads running through it. The geomancers were skilled astrologers, for not only had the earth's currents to be found but the influences of the planets also considered. The planets related to the five elements or materials (earth, water, fire, wood and metal) and the shapes of the hills. Some of these were compatible with each other, and some were not. Thus, if the natural shapes of hills were incorrect, the Chinese would physically alter them by pointing tops with cairns, or depressing them until they had produced a perfectly balanced landscape. This subject has been studied in detail and is described by John Michell in *View Over Atlantis* (1969).

In Britain, and indeed throughout the world, the early inhabitants may too have engineered the landscape by removing obstacles which would have impeded the flow of power, or added features to make it perfect. Sacred places such as springs and wells may have been linked by alignments of stones and hill ridges to circles and cromlechau and mounds which formed power centres for the earth current.

The removal of Britain's ancient structures and stones in the past may have upset the balance of power in the same way as one faulty bulb in the Christmas tree lights will put the whole string out of action. Certain old houses have been destroyed by fire over and over again through the centuries or the owners dogged by bad luck; some people think that this, and indeed Accident Black Spots, could have been caused by ignorant altering of the landscape.

Underground streams, or the veins of the earth, may have been kept healthy by standing stones containing quartz which united heaven and earth. In the same way an acupuncture practitioner helps the body to heal itself by inserting needles to balance the forces of Yin and Yang within it. Dowsers have practised acupuncture of the land successfully in recent years, when so-called black streams running under houses have affected the health and fate of people living in them.

It is said the earliest writings on acupuncture in China go back 4,500 years. The first needles were made of bone, bamboo and stone, perhaps jade or precious stone, and were described as stone piercers or borers and used by a doctor named Yu Fu. *The Book of the Mountains and Seas* written over 2,000 years ago mentioned rich deposits of jade in the Kaoshih mountains underlaid with stone suitable for making needles. There was a mention in the *Canon of Medicine* that abscesses were best treated with a small sharp-edged stone flake or needle.

It is not only suggested that the Stone Age people knew how to arrange the landscape so that it was most advantageous to them, but, as previously said, the practice was continued until the Reformation in the building of churches and houses. Thus many sites have been occupied by buildings of one sort or another by intent rather than accident for thousands of years.

It is certain that many parish churches are built on mounds, barrows, within earthworks, over standing stones; on the continent there is an example of a cromlech in the transept of a church. It is complete with upright and two capstones.

Near Aberystwyth a church has almost definitely been built within a stone circle and there are possible sites elsewhere in Dyfed. Alfred Watkins quoted many examples in *The Old Straight Track*; with reference to churches being built on ancient stones he suggested that there are probably many unseen ones built into the fabric of old churches. There are examples of standing stones in churchyards, one at Llanddewi Brefi, and ancient carved crosses of the Nevern type may have developed from simpler stones. The tessellated pavement of a Roman villa forms the floor of the tiny isolated church of Widford in Oxfordshire. People have wondered why churches were built miles away from any habitation. Cases like this may point to the idea of keeping the site right by building a church on it even if it was not needed by a village.

Standing stones have been built into houses in recent years as at Tremaenhir, Whitchurch, but there are probably many unknown stones hidden in walls. A plumber told of finding one barring his way when trying to make a hole in a wall for a waterpipe. Farms were probably built within stone circles as was the village of Avebury; the evidence from the farm of Glynsaithmaen, Mynachlog-ddu indicates a similar situation.

Cross Roads and Stone Names

When searching for ancient stones, place names are found to be of the greatest importance. In Wales the old names have survived to a large extent and are of extreme interest, being largely descriptive of the places. Named cross roads are easy to pick out on O.S. maps and more are on old tithe maps, farm maps, or remembered verbally. Wherever the word cross (or *groes*) appears, even though it is at a farm or house now away from main roads, it is significant. In the Northern hill region of Pembrokeshire the words *maen* (stone) or post or *iet* (gate) appear more frequently at cross roads possibly because these areas were less populated and the Christian word cross was less likely to be applied to stones at cross roads. Ordnance Survey maps of Pembrokeshire mark only a few of the cross names, amongst which are Longstone, Gilfach, Molleston, Scollock, Sampson, Newton, Hayscastle, Wallaston, Robeston, Nolton, Henner, Spittal, Lady's, Bill, Rogeston, Tiers, Simpson, Tref Asser, Pelcomb, Dinas, St Nicholas, Redstone (compare with Post Goch in the north of the county). Then in Welsh there are Croes-goch, Croes Llanfyrn, Croes Philip, Croes Wdig, Croes Wen, Croes Fihangel, Croes y Forwyn, Croesffordd Llannerch, Maen-y-groes, Tre-groes, Pant-y-groes, Bwlch-y-groes, Nant-y-groes; the English names appear of Crosswell, Cross Way, Cross Inn Farm, Cross House and Cross Land.

Ancient sites frequently line up with cross roads and where these have not been opened up as a traffic safeguard, ancient stones can sometimes be found embedded in hedgebanks or perhaps beneath tarmac. Churches are often found at crossing points on ley lines, having been built on sites of ancient stones, which are probably incorporated into the foundations. Churchyard crosses have been found to have ancient stones at their bases or may have been actually carved from standing stones as can be seen in Brittany. Alfred Watkins, writing about these and mark stones, noted four in a straight line visible from one place. He thought, in addition the ceremony of laying foundation stones with coins and mementos beneath was a survival of important buildings being sited on mark stones which also had deposits below them. In some cases a Roman altar has been used for the same purpose.

Once straight roads have twisted off course through the centuries, but it appears they always right themselves again at the old crossing points, though nowadays these may have been shifted to prevent accidents, and old mark stones may be still in place some yards away from the present crossing. Through history these crossing places have had great importance as gathering points for proclamations, cures, preaching and markets. More sinister uses which come to mind are burial places for suicides, murderers or witches, often with a stake through the heart. The bodies of these people were not allowed to be buried in consecrated ground so presumably interment at a crossing point would allow evil spirits to disperse away from habitation. Old traditions die hard. Fresh flowers are placed regularly on an isolated cross roads in the Cotswolds which is known as Betty's grave.

If warts were counted and the same number of pebbles put in a bag and deposited at a cross roads, the warts would be transferred to the person who picked up the bag.

Funerals stopped at cross roads and prayers were said. Apparitions such as headless horsemen, witches and the Devil have been seen in these places.

At midnight on All Hallows Eve circ. 1858 women in the Tenby area would gather at the cross road haunts of spirits to sow hemp. A vision of their loved one would appear and rake in the seed. Hemp and hallucinating were not illegal in those days.

Wherever stone appears in a place name, it can be safely assumed an important stone once stood there, (in some cases it still does, as at Haroldston) though some scholars would have us believe ton comes from the Anglo-Saxon word *tun* meaning habitation. However, in the 'English' parts of Pembrokeshire, where this influence would be strong, there is evidence of stones having existed: three long stones at Robeston, two at Druidston, four at Letterston, and others at Gumfreston, Clarbeston, Bletherston, Herbrandston, Hubberston, Jordanston, while at Loveston people played games around the stone. Puncheston still has a marvellous stone in the village. Other stone names in Pembrokeshire are Ambleston and Boulston which suggest legends of movement, also Bosherston, Cosherston, Hodgeston, Williamston, Yerbeston, Johnston, Granston, Lambston and Wiston.In the Welsh-speaking part of the county, the name Maen crops up less frequently, and more in farm names. Maenclochog had many more stones that it boasts today. I painted stones at Tre Maenhir, Ty'n Meini, Bryn Meini, Dolau Maen, and Glynsaithmaen. Once there were stones at Maen Llwyd, Blaen Meini and Maen Gwyn Hir. Other places where probably stones were to be found are Maen Post, Rhos Maen, Post Gwyn, Maen Saison, Pant-y-maen Sel, Maen Dewi, Maen Coch, Pen Maen, Pont Bren Maen, Glyn Maen, Maen Hir and Garreg Wen.

All these stones were probably of great importance where through the centuries people met in the open air for legislative counts, fairs, feasts and dances. As time passed villages grew up round some and others fell into disuse.

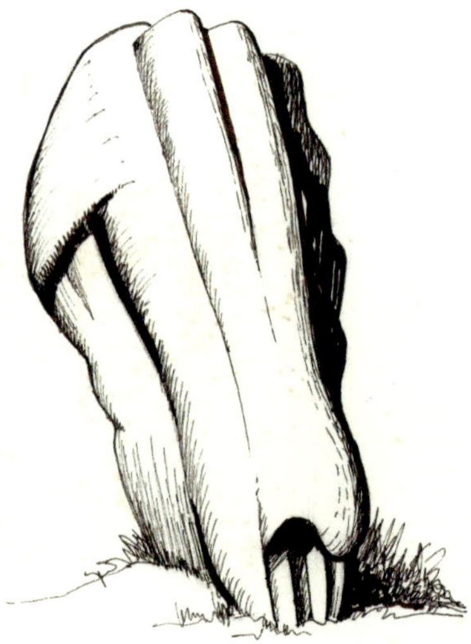

Folk Lore: Giants

Perhaps the answer to the movement of stones can be found in folk lore.

There are many ancient worldwide traditions about stones flying from place to place. Countless explanatory tales of ancient stones being moved by giants may be the remnants of this belief. Geoffrey of Monmouth told of Merlin's helpers trying to move the Blue Stones from the Ring in Ireland and being unable to do so in spite of ropes and ladders. Merlin, however, moved them with no trouble and re-erected them on Salisbury Plain 'by his artistry'. They were said to have had healing properties and to have been carried originally to Ireland from Africa by a race of giants. A similar tale was told of the stones of Callanish which were said to have been brought and set up by a King and a large company of Africans.

A stone near Cwm Cerwyn was said to have been thrown by Arthur, while the Tibble Stone near Tewkesbury was said to have been dropped by a giant as he was carrying it to destroy his neighbour's house. A giant wanted to destroy Hereford Cathedral but the stone he threw fell short and landed in a field. Two stones on the Morfa in Nevern Parish were said to have been dropped when they were being taken to build Trelly-faint Cromlech. They were used as gateposts and now there is only one left.

Giants liked to play bowls but forgot to pick up one called the Bowl Rock in Cornwall. Others threw stones from Cardiganshire to Ireland. The Devil and Jack O'Kent were having a stone-throwing competition and the stones landed at Trellech, Gwent. A giant threw his stick after his dog and it stuck in the ground at Maen y Bardd, Ro-wen, Gwynedd: it is also called Arthur's Spear. Names of standing stones such as the Devil's Quoit speak for themselves. There is Carreg Coetan near Puncheston.

Saints were also said to throw stones. A large white quartz standing stone which used to be on the parish boundary near Llanfyrnach was said to have been thrown from the summit of Frenni Fawr by St Samson but the quoit at Sampson's Farm and the two others at Stackpole are called Devil's Quoits. St Samson lifted the capstone of Longhouse cromlech with his little finger. St Fechan lifted the 2½ ton lintel over a church doorway. A large stone known as Marbel Samson is near a tumulus in Cilgerran parish.

Flight

It was supposed to be very difficult to move stones from their positions, except in the cases of holy men such as St Patrick who not only moved mountains but transported a leper to Ireland on an altar of stone; St Brynach carried the stone cross in Nevern churchyard across the Irish Sea on his shoulder.

Legends tell not only of giants and saints throwing stones, but of men flying on them as did the leper. Simon Magus, the magician who wished to buy the power of the Holy Spirit from St Peter, invented a flying wheel with the help of Mog Ruith, the Irish Archdruid. It crashed and its remnants were taken back from Italy to Tipperary by the Druid's daughter who erected them as a pillar stone. So powerful were the remains of the flying wheel that they caused blindness or death if looked at or touched.

Moving Churches

There are legends of mounds appearing suddenly as one did when St David was preaching at Llanddewi Brefi. When he found his voice could not be heard by the large congregation he caused the ground to rise under his feet. On that mound the church was subsequently built.

Tales of churches being moved overnight by unseen hands may originate in the idea that Christian sites were planned by geomancers in the same way as prehistoric monuments. If they were being built in the 'wrong' place, they had to be moved to make the landscape 'right', and particularly those which were started in valleys and were taken up to hilltops. An exception to this was a site called Yr Hen Eglwys (*the old church*), a collection of boulders which could be seen on the road side on the way to Porth Mawr beach, St David's. This was said to be the place where the first church was started, but every night the day's work was removed, until the site was changed to that of the present cathedral.

Countless legends on the same theme occur in Britain, amongst which are Churchdown in Gloucestershire where the Devil moved stones from the selected site at the bottom, to the top of the chosen hill. Alfred Watkins quotes three churches and a house in Herefordshire which were moved invisibly overnight during construction. In Wales various unseen hands moved the beginnings of churches at Llangar, Meirionnydd; Corwen, Denbighshire; Capel Garmon, Aberconwy; Wrexham; Llanbister; Llangelor; Maros; Llangan; Llanwinio; Llanddeusant; Llanddewi Brefi; Penbryn; and Llanfihangel Genau'r Glyn. Various legends explain the re-siting of these churches.

Dancing Stones

Monoliths have a rich folk lore, much of which is connected with the idea of their ability to move on their own. Much legend was lost in recent centuries as people became better educated in the modern sense, and certain religious bodies connected folk lore with idolatry.

Stones were reputed to dance at certain times of the year. The Devil's Quoits at St Petroc's went down to the River to dance; the Waterstone at Wrington dances when there is a full moon on Midsummer's Day; the Nine Maidens on Belstone Common move or dance daily at noon; Wimblestone near Shipham in Somerset dances in the moonlight; Carreg Lleidr in Anglesey runs round its field three times when the clock strikes twelve at Christmas. Giraldus told a story of a stone known as the thigh bone because it was of similar shape. If moved, it would always return to its position. Hugh, Earl of Chester had it chained to another stone and thrown into the sea to test its powers of movement. The next day it was back in its original position again. The stones at Duffryn in Glamorganshire whirled round and curtsied on Midsummer's Eve. One of the names for Stonehenge is the Giant's Dance.

The circle cult in connection with standing stones seems all important in prehistory and folk lore, in which relics of it appear frequently. It has obvious associations with the sun and moon, and observances took place at particular times of the year, coming down to us in children's circle games.

In Scotland James VI condemned the spread of witchcraft in the early seventeenth century, and a ritual which was known as Raising the Power. Some people think its purpose was to build up and store the power of the earth's currents, and that the expending of human energy in the form of vigorous running, dancing or even crawling in circles, mostly round standing stones, was in some way instrumental in doing this. In folk customs countless examples occur, especially at the solstice and equinoctial festivals, and at seasons of the full moon. Usually multiples of three were required in the running, and this had to be done with the sun.

On May morning a well at Tullybelton (Beltane?) was drunk from by people who then walked nine times round it and then the standing stones nearby. Going nine times round the stone at Sennon brought good luck; a wayside cross on top of a tumulus was once walked round three times each year in Warwickshire on November 11th at sunrise. Walking nine times round a fairy path at full moon would reveal the entrance to fairyland. Children ran in and out of alternate stones of the circle at Gors Fawr before they could pass between the pair of standing stones nearby. Incidentally it was supposed that fairies had particular associations with standing stones which were the gates to fairyland and were said to glow at certain seasons.

A story was told in Pembrokeshire of a shepherd boy who on a misty day became lost in the hills. After walking for hours he found himself in a hollow where there were streams and rushes, and immediately recognised it as a dangerous place because of the rings. He could not get out of the place however hard he tried, and was then met by a man with bright blue eyes who took him to a standing stone. He tapped on it three times and lifted it up, revealing beneath it a flight of steps leading to a beautiful subterranean world lit by a magical blue light. He lived there for some time and married a fairy wife whom he later took back with him to the human world. She bore him a son, Taliesin, the renowned bard. This is only one of the stories of his origin.

In Brittany the Corrigans or dwarfs are believed to dance round *meini hirion*, and it is thought that the surviving circular dances of that country are the remnants of an initiatory sun ceremony which took place at the numerous stones.

The Gorsedd has similarities in its connection with stones and the sun.

Other survivals of running round stones might be the beating of parish boundaries, which were marked with stones in past centuries, and dancing round maypoles. The latter were possibly substitutes for standing stones, and in some districts a white birch tree was used as a pole. At Tenby the townspeople danced from decorated pole to pole, threading the needle at each. This is reminiscent of the practice of running in and out of the stones at Gors Fawr. At Durrington in Wiltshire on old May Day villagers danced round a pole which was chained to the Cross stones, so in this the two types of post were combined. Maypoles were often placed on high places.

The Whitsun ram sales at Kingsteinton in Devon were accompanied by maypole dancing, and a procession carrying a decorated dead lamb which was afterwards roasted and eaten. This might have been a sacrificial survival.

Maypole festivities appear to have originated in the all important Beltane fire and sun observances, at May and Midsummer, and continued in various forms through the centuries. All ages and classes of society including royalty dressed poles as tall as 134 ft in flowers and leaves, and danced round them with great merrymaking. In the Commonwealth all such frivolities were suppressed. They were re-introduced at the Restoration but again declined until made popular again in their present form by Ruskin in the late nineteenth century with child May queens and ribbon-plaiting dances.

The following customs are almost certainly connected with fertility rites:

People would dance round stones to have wishes answered and this idea was connected with the practice of running a certain number of times (it was frequently a multiple of three) round a church and putting a finger in the keyhole. In Montgomeryshire on St John's Eve if girls wished to discover the identity of their future husbands it was necessary to walk nine and a half times round the church ending at the door, when a 'diviner' would place a knife in the keyhole saying 'here is the knife, where is the sheath?'. In Anglesey a drawn sword was carried three times round the church pointing it at the door with each revolution. On the fourth time the true love (or the Devil) would take hold of the scabbard. It is possible that these churches were built on sites of ancient stones as many were. On All Hallows Eve a person would leave the house holding a glove and walk nine times round it saying 'Here's the glove, where's the hand?', hoping to see the face of his sweetheart. In Cardiganshire it was the dung heap that was chosen to walk nine times round chanting 'here's the shoe, where's the foot?' and in Carmarthenshire it was the leek bed! In the Vale of Glamorgan again the church was chosen and the person who wished to find the identity of his sweetheart would turn his coat inside out, recite the Lord's Prayer backwards, walk round the church and put his finger in the keyhole of the door.

Another custom in which nine figured was held on May Eve in the Vale of Glamorgan when nine men removed all money and metal from their persons and collected wood from nine different kinds of trees. Then one or two circles were cut in the ground and fires built within them, the people standing round watching. Brown and white cakes were broken in four, put in a bag and each person had to take a piece. Those who took brown pieces had to jump three times over the fires or run three times between if there were two, thus ensuring a good harvest.

Nine holes drilled in a mutton shoulderblade bone which was placed under the pillow would insure a dream of the future partner, in the Tenby area.

Marks on Stones

Folk lore attributes marks on certain stones to historical events. In Pembrokeshire the altar stone at St Non's chapel was said to bear the imprints of the saint's fingers when she held it during the birth of St David in a thunderstorm.

Rocks on the island of Skomer were marked by the hooves of St David's horse. A stone at Pumsaint is said to bear the marks of the feet of the five saints. The marks of a giant's finger and thumb can be seen on the stone he threw to Maentwrog, Gwynedd. Giant's finger marks can be seen on the Tibble stone near Tewkesbury.

Growing

It was widely believed that stones were capable of growth and that they even multiplied. At Blaxhall in Suffolk there is a magical growing stone. A ploughman turned it up and carried it to the farmyard where it started growing. It is now six to eight feet long. Some people say it came from Lincolnshire in the Ice Age. It is not hard for anyone who has been engaged in clearing stones from land to believe they grow. Pudding stones were also believed to multiply.

Washing and Drinking Stones

Stones were said to move to streams to wash or drink. The Fishstone at Crickhowell is said to swim in the Usk on Midsummer's Eve; Maen Llia moves to the river Nedd at cockcrow; Four stones at Old Radnore drink at a pool when the church bells ring; the Giant's Stone on Ronsay drinks from the loch on New Year's morning; at the same time the Stane O'Quoybune on Birsay also drinks from the loch. On May morning the Motty Stone on Cronebane Hill goes to wash. The Druidstone near Michaelstone-y-Fedw swims in the river if a cock crows at night.

Petrifaction

Some monoliths are connected with stories of petrifaction for various reasons, many of which are about dancing on the Sabbath. The stories of actual stones dancing may have been altered as a lesson in Sunday observance. Stones round the cromlech called Tinkinswood Burial Chamber in South Glamorgan are said to be women who were turned to stone for dancing on a Sunday. A pillar of limestone near Clydach, Gwent, is supposed to be a shepherd, petrified because of his cruelty to his wife. The stones of the circle of Boscawen-Un are said to be nine maidens turned to stone for Sunday dancing. There are other nine maidens, pipers and fiddlers, hurlers, and witches like Long Meg and her daughters in Cumbria. Perhaps the most famous of these standing stones are at Rollright: the king, his soldiers and the whispering knights.

Fertility

Many large stones were connected with fertility rites, as were stones with holes which were big enough to put fingers through. They were also used to help women in labour.

At Carnac in Brittany women wishing to conceive would go to Le Grand Menhir Brise on May 1st. As late as 1917 another stone at Carnac was cut down because the ceremonies performed there were thought improper.

The holed stone at Doagh, Ireland, attracted newly married couples who clasped hands through the hole. A stone in Orkney with similar associations was destroyed in 1814. In the Isle of Man couples clasped hands through stone rings in the churchyard during wedding ceremonies. In the Scilly Isles there is a stone with a hole in it through which engaged couples would join hands.

Certain stones were sat on by infertile women: the Bride's Chair in Lancashire; Branham Wood, Ross and Cromarty; Kings Park, Edinburgh.

The famous Aphrodite stone at Paphos, Cyprus was kept veiled by its priests because it was supposed to be too holy to be seen. The Emperor Theodosius abolished the cult in the fourth century, but even today candles are lit and offerings placed in a small hole in the corner stone of the ruined temple. The symbol of a cone-shaped stone appears on ancient coins from Cyprus.

Rocking Stones

Some rocking stones are said to be connected with fertility rites, especially where they were sited on coasts. They were huge, delicately placed boulders which rocked when touched, but most have been destroyed by vandals through the centuries. Some have been replaced but not sufficiently skilfully to recreate their rocking ability. Three Pembrokeshire examples on Skomer, St David's Head and Trellwyn Fawr, Llanllawer have all been overthrown; the one at St David's Head was upset in the Civil War. At the same time a Cornish rocking or logan stone was displaced, and few of the many which still exist are capable of rocking now.

These enormous blocks are poised on their supporting rocks with such precision that in one case it was said to be possible to crack nuts beneath it. They have fascinated people through the centuries. Many coastal rocking stones are carved with cup marks and terminate alignments of ancient sites. Alfred Watkins described the Buckstone in the Forest of Dean which he considered to be a natural feature, but noted a

deliberately carved basin in a rock nearby. He considered it might have been made to hold burning fat for sacrificial purposes, and perhaps connected with beacon light.

Fenton mentions three rocking stones together on Plumstone Mountain, and one near Sealyham House as well as that on St David's Head.

Healing Stones

Stones in Britain and other parts of the world are associated with healing. Sometimes they are flat topped, and sometimes they have holes through which people crawled or thrust their limbs.

Those with holes were supposed to have power to cure rheumatism, rickets and other diseases. A stone shaped like a wheel between two standing stones in Cornwall is called the Men-an-Tol stone. Rheumatism sufferers crawled through a hole in a stone in the parish of Aghade in order to prevent or cure rickets. The Speckled Stone at Tobernavean near Sligo has an oblong-shaped hole through which diseased children were once pushed.

Stones with hollows in which rain water collected were said to be good for various cures. The water was used for washing in or drunk as a medicine.

Geoffrey of Monmouth tells of Merlin's advice to move the Giant's Ring (Stonehenge) from Ireland to England; how all the stones had healing properties, and the giants poured water over the stones into baths in which they washed the sick so they should be cured. The Aubrey Holes are too far away from the majority of the stones to have been used for this purpose, but there are two other circles of holes nearer which could perhaps have been used as baths. The idea of water being poured over stones has been mentioned in connection with quartz. In the seventeenth century a stone near Baud in Brittany called the Venus de Quinipilly had a stone trough at its base in which the sick were cured, and young people bathed as a fertility rite.

In county Durham there is a stone which cures rheumatism and pains in the limbs when sick people sit on it. There is at least one stone in Pembrokeshire with a flat top which has curative powers.

Small stones of various types were used for healing and some were beautifully mounted. A stone shaped like a knuckle bone was kept in a pillar cross and was taken to the houses of ill people, always being replaced in the cross afterwards, presumably so that it could be recharged with energy. Small charm stones were placed in water which was afterwards drunk. Certain stones were curative if rubbed on wounds. In Carmarthenshire a ball of a soft stone as big as a man's head was scraped and the ensuing powder mixed with water and drunk as a preventative against rabies. A person who took this water described an extraordinary sensation as if the blood was boiling in her veins.

The original cap of St Olan's stone Co. Cork was said to be a cure for feminine ailments. If put on the head and carried round the church three times it cured headaches. It also returned to its position by itself.

Fishermen had weather stones to which they would bring offerings for fair weather. Iona stones were carried in pouches round the neck as a charm against drowning. Certain of St Columba's monks were said to be learned in the healing properties of stones; but Iona is so full of stone lore as to be a study in itself. In the Admiralty charts of Iona an entry in 1969 warned it was not safe to rely on the magnetic compass on that coast as there was too much interference from the local stones.

There are records of the curious practice of burying people alive for a period of time as a cure for madness, physical illness or to avert a curse that had been laid. Presumably the power of the earth's current was being used as a cure, rather than that of a stone. In all cases the sufferer was totally buried except for the head. The recipe must have been badly distorted in the story of the wife who was buried up to the neck by her husband as a punishment. No one was allowed to go near her except her sister who gave her sustenance from the dew which collected on the hem of her trailing skirt. Needless to say a phantom white lady haunted the spot afterwards. A similar idea occurred in Wales on Shrove Tuesday if an unlucky hen failed to produced eggs for pancakes; it was taken out into a field, a turf was cut, and the hen buried up to its neck until the next day, when it was killed and eaten with much ceremony.

This may be the correct place to add the well known story of St Patrick at the stone circle at Mag Slecht, County Cavan. He found the chief idol decorated with silver and gold and the twelve others with brass. As he went to place his crozier on the chief idol it turned over on its side, and the twelve others were swallowed up in the earth as far as their heads to remain as an example.

Veneration of Stones

The Aphrodite stone has been mentioned already and with this in mind the troubles of the early Church can be recalled. Ancient sites had been allowed to remain and churches built in or upon them; stones had been Christianised by baptism and inscriptions cut upon them. The trouble of stone veneration continued still, particularly in France with its great wealth of stones. At Arles in AD 452 an edict was issued stating it was sacrilegious to worship trees, stones, torches or fountains. In AD 567 The Council of Tours that excommunication should be the penalty for the same practices. The Pope sent a message in AD 601 telling St Augustine to have idols smashed, but to preserve the temples and have them sprinkled with holy water to purify them from Devil worship. Bishops at Nantes were ordered to dig up and hide stones where they could not be found, as earlier efforts had been ineffective. However, in spite of all this, the practice continued and remnants of it can be found in British folk lore.

In Narberth parish a square stone used to stand in a hedge until it fell into a lane. It was considered unlucky to pass by without touching it.

The Lady Stone at Ty'n meini Farm was an object of respect, and passengers passing by in the coach would raise their hats to it in greeting.

Initiation Stones

One of Britain's most famous stones is the Stone of Scone beneath the Coronation chair in Westminster Abbey. Sovereigns have been crowned on it since Edward I brought it from Scone Abbey in Scotland where thirty-four Scottish Kings had been crowned previously. It was reputed to have been taken to Scone from Iona via Ireland, Spain, Egypt and Palestine.

The King Stone at Kingston-on-Thames was the seat on which Anglo-Saxon monarchs were crowned. Similar stones of initiation once existed, such as the

Stone of Kings, Tyrone; the Black Stones of Iona; the Stone of Inauguration on Islay, and the Chair of the O'Neill's of Castlereagh; or the Lia Fail at Tara, which some people say is still there, and others think is the Coronation Stone at Westminster.

A large stone known as the King's Table or Arthur's Table in the hilltop castle of Carn Fodron in Gwynedd is also reputed to be associated with the Westminster stone.

Some of these stones had marks in which the king would put his feet or hands; it was thought that he would draw power from the stone.

St Patrick was said to have seen his vision of Ireland from a huge stone in the chapel on the shore at Porth Mawr near St David's, in spite of the ground being too low there. It was known as St Patrick's Seat, but was removed centuries ago.

Oaths were sworn upon stones, proclamations were made and trading took place at them. Examples of these are the Black Stones of Iona and the London Stone in the City.

The nineteenth-century historians Jones and Freeman mentioned a very large stone on the Burrows near Porth Mawr; it was called Arthur's Stone and was carved with three parallel arched lines intersected by three parallel perpendicular lines. 'The Bishop of St Davids has twelve pence a year for the ten acres of land holden by that stone.' This was probably a different stone from the seat in the chapel.

There are numerous stone seats in Britain, some of which were sat upon for healing, or to induce fertility as well as those which were the seats of judges and kings. All these people were seeking the release of power from the stone for one reason or another.

Funeral Stones

At Whitchurch near Solva there was a squarish stone opposite the church gate where all funerals stopped while the body was carried round it. The dead were carried three times round a stone outside the churchyard gate at Brilley in Herefordshire: in order to prevent the Devil taking the soul.

At Formby in Lancashire bodies were carried round the Godstone three times so that the soul should not return to haunt relatives. In Devon this was done three times sunwise round the churchyard cross at Manaton. The vicar had the stone broken up and the fragments concealed to stop the practice.

At St David's, funerals would stop at the various crosses in the city, perhaps the remains of the custom of the pilgrims to the Shrine saying the Stations of the Cross at them. But it may of course have been harking back to earlier customs at standing stones.

Alfred Watkins recounted the moving of the old churchyard cross at Bosbury, Herefordshire, which revealed a huge boulder of puddingstone beneath it.

Ladi Wen

Ladi Wen (*white lady*) is often mentioned in Welsh folk lore. She is connected with the oldest traditions, and was a beautiful white phantom-like being who inhabited hills, tumuli, cromlechau, wells and stones. Perhaps she was the pure, shining, white being that came walking silently at dawn on Midsummer morning down the avenue of stones at Callanish. The local people went to visit them secretly, as they had been forbidden to go there by the ministers, and believed they had seen a god. Arthur's queen Gwenhwyfar seems to come from the same source.

In the *Mabinogion* the story of Pwyll, Prince of Dyfed is told. As he sat on the gorsedd or mound of Arberth he saw (a vision of) a beautiful lady in a garment of shining gold riding a pure white horse along the road that led to the mound. Three times Pwyll sent one of his companions to follow her but however hard he rode he could not catch up with her before she disappeared. She could have been the same shining being the people of Callanish awaited. Eventually Pwyll himself followed, called out, and caught up with her; from then on in the story she became an ordinary human woman.

Pembrokeshire as well as the rest of Britain has white lady places. She guarded the treasure at Lady's Gate, Llanwnda, and possibly the Lady Stone at Tynmeini, near Eglwyswrw, where there must have been more stones than the one broken survivor. She haunts Yet Wen (*white gate*). In the same small area are several more white names, Ffynnon Wen (*white well*), Garn Wen (*white cairn*), Ysgubor Wen (white barn), and Wen Allt (*white hill*).

Another reference comes from St Dogmael's where the Sagranus Stone, inscribed with Ogam marks and lettered, was said to have been used as a bridge before being placed in the church. A white lady and also the Devil were said to haunt it on the 'three spirit nights'.

On All Hallows Eve bonfires were lit and small stones thrown into them. In Anglesey a rhyme was sung which told of a headless white lady and a tailless black sow. In the morning people searched for the stones they had thrown in the fire the night before; if they found them they had good luck for the rest of the year.

Numerous wells were associated with the white lady. Near one in the Isle of Man there is a white quartz standing stone known as the White Lady of Ballafreer. A fertility rite was performed there by girls who filled their mouths with water from the well, and walked three times sunwise round the monolith before dawn. Then they swallowed the water, and said in the Manx language, 'In the Name of the Father, Son and Holy Ghost'.

Making It Right

In folk lore standing stones have often been connected with battles and fights. Perhaps these legends grew up centuries after they were set up when their purpose had been forgotten. An explanation was needed and it was assumed they were grave stones commemorating the burial places of heroes; this belief is still widespread. Though there are burials under some of them it is unlikely they were placed there for interment in the Christian sense. It seems more likely the burials, and they were usually cremated, were put below the stone with other offerings as a sacrifice: to make the stone right in some way. A similar practice was continued for centuries in the building of houses and churches, but animal bones were usually used instead of those of humans. When floors have been taken up in old Pembrokeshire houses horses skulls have been found buried beneath the four corners of the house. During the restoration of Steynton church in 1882 not only was a horse's skull found under the floor, but a human thigh bone was built into each of the pillars. Horses skulls were found in the Chapel at Caerfarchell. These practices seem to link up with tales of buried treasure and the belief that if a victim was killed and buried there the ghost would haunt the spot and frighten away treasure hunters.

Bad Luck

Legends continually mention bad luck overtaking stone movers. One of the best known must be that of the farmer from Rollright in Oxfordshire who despite warnings from neighbours decided to move a stone from the circle there, and in doing so broke his wagon and killed his four horses with the exertion. Bad luck overtook him until he had only one old horse and cart left. With no difficulty he got the stone in the cart and the half-dead horse pulled it up to the circle where he put it in its proper position; from then on his good luck returned.

A farmer in Lancashire moved the Written Stone from a lane into his dairy but was forced to replace it because of poltergeist activity. The same thing happened when a piece of broken stone was made into a doorstep. A similar occurrence of bad luck was recorded in Essex as recently as 1944 when a stone was moved. When it was replaced all was well again. When the owner of a stone tried to move it from its site in Lincolnshire, his four harnessed horses died with the extreme effort of this act of removal.

Associated with the inappropriate removal of stones are accounts of illness in cattle, deaths of horses and paralysis of men's limbs, and cattle refusing to enter a cowshed where a stone had been used as a lintel. Ghosts of stone movers haunted the places till the stones were replaced; thunder and lightning struck people down, the Devil or other terrible apparitions were seen and mysterious voices spoke from inside burial chambers. Countless stories of illness, bankruptcy and bad luck were warnings to others not to meddle with stones and so destroy the power places.

* * *

There are many more traditions associated with stones. As it was believed they were alive it was thought necessary to take oblations to them for various reasons; thank offerings were made for wishes granted, or sacrifices made to placate the stone if wrong had been done. Various foods such as cakes, honey or alcohol were put on stones, and milk and even the blood of animals poured into cup marks or depressions on them. Sometimes they were garlanded with flowers. These things were done on May Day, or Midsummer's Day. In Ireland, it was believed the cows would fail to milk if the offerings were forgotten.

Stones were thought to be lucky, and drovers chipped pieces from them to take away as talismans, but it was thought to be unlucky to try to count the stones of circles and that the same number could never be counted twice; or bad luck or death would strike the counter.

There were 'altars' of cursing stones; small pebbles in hollows on flat-topped stones were turned and curses pronounced.

If questions were asked of certain stones they were thought to give an answer in one way or another. They could tell where to find lost belongings or who were the thieves who had stolen them. The bridge arched over the Alun rivulet near the North door of St David's cathedral replaced a huge marble slab. It was 10 ft long, 6 ft wide, and 1 ft thick, and known as Llechllafar, the

Speaking Stone. Giraldus Cambrensis noted a crack across it which was said to have occurred as a protest when a corpse was carried over it. It also spoke or prompted people to prophesy.

Superstition and Science

As we have seen, it now seems widely accepted that there is some force or power in standing stones. Sensitive dowsers have detected bands of energy spiralling upwards through certain points in stones, and lines of charge shooting off for many miles across country. They have experienced various shock-like sensations and sometimes unpleasant reactions, but not at all times of the day or seasons of the year.

Work in a similar field but from a different angle has been carried out by Dr G. V. Robins of the Institute of Archaeology. In 1983 he described his work at the Rollright Circle in Oxfordshire, a favourite, enigmatic and much dowsed site, in which he used an ultrasonic detector to study sounds made by bats. He noticed that readings were still being registered after the bats had gone, so concluded waves were being emitted by the stones in the circle. The signals varied minute by minute, pulsing up and down, and being more powerful for two hours either side of sunrise. They were found to be strongest at the equinoxes and weakest at the solstices. In 1979 a round-the-clock, three-week survey was undertaken when radioactivity was measured by geigercounter. The readings between the circle and the outlying King Stone were three times higher than the ambient background although Dr Robins did not consider the natural below-surface rocks in that area were likely to be radioactive.

Circles studied in the same way in Cornwall produced much lower readings in comparison with Rollright, yet the rocks in those areas would have been expected to be more radioactive. He found this puzzling and needed more data for explanation. He wondered if the circle affected the site or the site affected the circle, and whether the people who set up the stones were more aware than we are of special places on the earth, and so marked them with stones.

It seems that his observations of Rollright have similarities to those of Tom Graves the dowser, particularly in connection with the circle and the King Stone, and may even corresponds with Professor Thom's suggestions about outlying standing stones.

Scientific discoveries are being made all the time, so it is possible that eventually the rediscovery will be made of forces and influences known to the megalith builders of which we are now unaware. For example, medicine has developed along different lines through the centuries, with Chinese acupuncture in one direction and European allopathic medicine in another, with the same end of healing in view.

This is a highly controversial subject, and when one is dealing with a civilisation which left no written records behind, one is forced into the area of supposition. It must be conceded there is much room for speculation and discovery.

> *Therefore judge nothing before the time, until the Lord come, who both will bring to light the hidden things of darkness, and will make manifest the counsels of the hearts: and then shall every man have praise of God.*
>
> I Corinthians, 4, verse 5

Cardigan
26 304089
Newport Bay
Fishguard Bay
34 304397
18 305171
3 413137
29 304345
53 413140
19 305198
Newport
35 276042
5 304049
46 305181
6 305160
4 304355
Fishguard
28 304325
36 304309
11 305175
27 413138
17 285
17 305175
31 304355
30 300423
33 304356
12 305192
24 304054
14 304108
32 413139
23 304065
1 413136
39 304362
43 305311
38 304361
9 304449
16 304064
40 305373
22 305214
37 304466
21 304454
15 304109
25 304281
13 275685
42 110339
20 304453
52 305316
41 305397
St David's
8 305325
Ramsey Island
PEMBROKESHIRE
St Brides Bay
Haverfordwest
7 305339
50 305372
44 305357
2 304235
Skomer Island
10 305351
Neyland
45 305354
Milford Haven
Saundersfoot
Skokholm Island
Pembroke Dock
Pembroke
Tenby
49 305410
48 305409
51 305411
Caldey Island
Carmarthen Bay
10 Painting Number
305354 National Principal Record Number
0 miles 5

Introduction

In the summer of 1981 I painted the series of 19th century Rubbing Stones at Manor Farm, Llanrhian. The visual experience of vertical shapes in a generally horizontal landscape was so engaging that I decided to search out and record, in a series of paintings, all the standing stones listed by Royal Commission on the Ancient and Historcal Monuments of Wales (RCAHMW) in the old county of Pembrokeshire.

As the project gathered momentum and the number of paintings grew, so did my enthusiasm for the subject. During the three years it took to complete the project, my husband and I became deeply involved with the subject of standing stones. Our days were spent discovering stones, reading and writing about them and I painted them in their landscapes. I painted every *maen hir* (standing stone) in the then current list compiled by the RCAHMW and we rediscovered some stones that were thought to have been lost. These marvellous sculptures in the landscape were, it seemed, unconsciously accepted and generally appreciated but little about them was understood by anyone. They were standing as they had for centuries, waiting for someone to re-discover their secret.

We decided they should be recorded pictorially and carefully examined. As much as possible should be discovered about their shapes and origins. We wanted to gather as many hypotheses on the subject as were available.

We covered most parts of the county in our searches and met many delightful people whom we termed the 'Keepers of the stones'. They could hardly be called owners, as generations of people disappear like dust in the wind when compared with the stones which may have been standing in their places for thousands of years.

Searching for stones, sometimes in vain, we climbed heather covered hillsides, scrambled over boulders, negotiated streams, muddy tracks and gateways. We searched for hours, sometimes walking unnecessary miles only to find the 'keepers' were out and so made return visits. We set off in the early morning, hoped for a good painting light and had various encounters whilst I painted and drew. The day could be filled with interruptions and meetings. We came upon interesting buildings, beautiful trees, rare wild flowers, varieties of local rock and soil types. There were of course people, who would discuss farming, tell us folk tales and on one occasion, whilst in the mountains, recruited our help with sheep mustering.

As I painted, inquisitive cattle, with their clouds of flies, might crowd between me and my subject: the stone. Galloping ponies and wandering sheep would sometimes become part of the composition of my painting. At times, we were chilled by wind and rain, at others, sun burned or threatened by thunder and lightning on the mountains or by the sea, but none of this was enough to dispel from these lovely places, the deep and abiding sense of peace.

Jill Young

List of Parishes in which the stones stand and the sites

	Page	**Parish**	**Sites**
1.	39	Llanrhian	Mr C Jenkins, Manor House, Llanrhian
2.	40	Amroth	Perrott's Wall, Nr Ludchurch
3.	43	Dinas	Pen Cnwc, Dinas
4.	44	Dinas	Tŷ Rhos, Dinas
5.	47	Eglwyswrw	Pant-y-Garn, Eglwyswrw
6.	48	Fishguard South	Ty'n Meini, Dinas Cross
7.	51	Haroldston West	St Catherines, Haroldston
8.	52	Hayscastle	Rhyndaston, Hayscastle
9.	55	Henry's Moat	Goetty Uchaf, Rosebush
10.	56	Hubberston	Dale Bay Farms Ltd, St Botolph's Mansion
11.	59	Jordanston	Clegyrn, Letterston
12.	60	Llanfair-Nant-y-Gof	Llygadcleddau, nr Tre-cŵn
13.	63	Llanfyrnach	Bryn Meini, Llanfyrnach
14.	64	Llanfyrnach	Nant-y-Groes, Llanfyrnach
15.	67	Llanfyrnach	Rhyd-y-Gath, Llanfyrnach
16.	68	Llangolman	Glynsaithmaen, Mynachlog Ddu
17.	71	Llanllawer	Trellwyn Fawr, Llanllawer
18.	73	Llanwnda	Glas Fryn, Llanwnda
19.	74	Llanwnda	Gilfach Farm, Goodwick
20.	77	Maenclochog	Galchen Farm, Maenclochog
21.	78	Maenclochog	Tynewydd, Maenclochog
22.	81	Mathry	Tynewyddgrug, Wolfscastle
23.	82	Mynachlog-ddu	Cwm Garw Common, Mynachlog-ddu
24.	85	Mynachlog-ddu	Dolau Maen, Mynachlog-ddu
25.	86	Mynachlog-ddu	Gors Fawr Common, Mynachlog-ddu
26.	99	Moylegrove	Trefais, Moylegrove
27.	90	Nevern (Nanhyfer)	Brynawel, Newport
28.	93	Nevern	Cilgwyn, Newport
29.	94	Nevern	Gellifawr, Newport
30.	97	Nevern	Waun Mawn Common, Nevern
31.	98	Nevern	Waun Mawn Common, Nevern
32.	101	Nevern	Tafarn-y-Bwlch Common, Nevern

	Page	Parish	Sites
33.	102	Nevern	Tafarn-y-Bwlch Common, Nevern
34.	105	Nevern	Trellyffaint, Newport
35.	106	Newport (Trefdraeth)	Carn Ingli Common, Newport
36.	109	Newport	Hendre, Newport
37.	110	Puncheston (Casnewydd-bach)	7, Council Houses, Puncheston
38.	113	Puncheston	Church Farm, Puncheston
39.	114	Puncheston	Fagwyr Frân West, Puncheston
40.	117	St David's (Tyddewi)	Drws Gobaith, St David's
41.	118	St David's	Trecenny, St David's
42.	121	St Dogwell's (Llandudoch)	Lower Broadmoor, Letterston
43.	122	St Edrins	Trehale, Mathry
44.	125	St Ishmael's	Sandyhaven House, St Ishmaels
45.	126	St Ishmael's	Trewarren House, St Ishmaels
46.	129	St Nicholas	Ffynnon Derwyddon, St Nicholas
47.	130	St Nicholas	Trefelgarn, St. Nicholas
48.	133	St Petrog's	Home Farm, Stackpole
49.	134	St Petrog's	Sampson Farm, Stackpole
50.	137	Skomer	Harold Stone, Skomer Island
51.	138	Stackpole Elidor	National Trust, Stackpole
52.	141	Whitchurch	Crowswood, Solva
53.	142	Nevern	Rhos Maen, Newport

Gill Young

LLANRHIAN PARISH (1)

Mr C Jenkins, Manor House, Llanrhian

(SM 819 315) NPRN 413136 NGR

The beautiful rubbing stones in the fields surrounding the manor house, church and village were the start of the collection.

From each of their sites are perfect views of the coastal scenery. They stand fairly centrally in the tidy fields of the well farmed land which was not enclosed until the last century.

Seven of the eight tall stones were certainly erected by a relative of the present owner. They were cut and taken from a quarry at Henllys, a short distance to the north of the farm, between 1850 and 1860. They were slung by rope between a pair of cartwheels and hauled to the places where they now stand. The holes and drill marks made in the quarrying and splitting of the slate can still be seen in the narrow pillars, the tallest of which is 108 inches high.

The eighth stone is different from the others in character and may be a natural boulder. It is not composed of slate, its many facets are lichen-covered, and in comparison with the others it is short and thick. It stands in a field known as Parc y Garreg (*stone field*).

AMROTH PARISH (2)

Perrott's Wall, Nr Ludchurch

(SN 146 096) NPRN 304235

The Longstone appears to be the only remaining listed stone in the south-eastern corner of Pembrokeshire and once must have been of strong significance, standing as it does near the junction of five ways. With the Mynydd Preseli in view, it is on a line which can be traced on the map from coast to coast, through King's Park and Prince's Gate, both possible sites of now missing pairs of stones. The legend of royal burials beneath *meini hirion* lingers in such place names.

The stone stands on the slope of a hill and being now 54 inches in height is shorter by 18 inches than when recorded by Royal Commission. There may be a considerable amount of the stone below ground as constant ploughing could have caused erosion by slipping of soil from the slope. It does not appear to have been fired or broken recently as the shape of its top is quite typical. It is composed of the most beautiful pink and apricot coloured quartz conglomerate containing lava-like rock. It has the smoothness and appearance of alabaster. It is laminated, looking as if it could be easily split along the lines of cleavage but is extremely hard and it appears to be unbroken and undamaged.

In spite of its preservation no local legends could be found except the knowledge that on no account must it be moved.

DINAS PARISH (3)

Pen Cnwc

(SN 386 002) NPRN 413 137

The Royal Commission survey mentions a stone 43 inches high in a field called Parc y Garreg (*stone field*). The list printed in the Pembrokeshire Historian 1966 states this stone could not be found. However it is still there, though since 1925 it has sunk and now measures only 30 inches, thus being below the height of mowing grass or standing corn. It is possible that the land is wet, or has built up around it due to cultivation as in many other cases, particularly on slopes. The search was well worth while as it revealed the beautiful top of a large, four-sided and obviously ancient stone, absolutely typical in shape. It has the usual flat back, wedge-shaped top to the wide sides, and a sloping front with a step towards the lower end in which are five apparently purpose-made indentations. The top, much rounded with age, has interesting depressions which were obviously made centuries ago.

It is possible that there is a tumulus in the corner of the same field, but of a later date than the stone.

DINAS PARISH (4)

Tŷ Rhos, Dinas

(SN 008 387) NPRN 304 335

Belonging to the type of slab-shaped monoliths, this one stands about 90 inches high, is 57 inches across at its widest part, and only a few inches thick. It is similar in shape to stones on the farms of Trewarren House, St Ishmaels; Sampson Farm, Stackpole; Stackpole Warren; Nant-y-Groes, Llanfyrnach; and Drws Gobaith, St David's.

The *maen hir* stands in a field on the most interesting site, the ground of which slopes gently upwards from the road, until it reaches a bank above the stone. The field name, Parc Cerrig Hirion implies there were once more stones there, and when seen in drought conditions it becomes obvious that many large stones have been tipped over and buried round the remaining one and on the bank above it. This was the custom on some farms in order to clear a larger area for cultivation. Aerial photography in suitable conditions, and also expert dowsing, would probably reveal more information here and in adjoining fields. This seems to be a site which would well repay excavation (though not for the owner) as all the stones, and possibly the existing one, have been moved.

The stone has been named after the Black Horse Inn which used to be the last house of the terrace beside the field, but has not been licensed in living memory according to a neighbour aged seventy years old. She remembered her mother talking of an inn at the end of the terrace. The name Black Horse has interesting connections. Currently named Lloyds Bank, the Black Horse Bank was a drover's bank but was formerly named the Black Ox Bank. Inns named after either of these animals were usually associated with livestock drovers and often acted as way stations on drovers' roads.

Jill Young

Jill Young

EGLWYSWRW PARISH (5)

Pant-y-Garn, Eglwyswrw

(SM 136 379) NPRN 304 049

The pathetic remains of this once gigantic stone known in the plural as Cerrig-y-Derwyddon (*druid's stones*) stand bravely erect to bear evidence to the destruction that took place in the last century. As the field name refers to stones in the plural there were obviously more at one time.

The Royal Commission survey recorded the stone had at one time stood 120 inches high above the ground, but had been blasted and the upper portion 'thrown into the hedge'. Careful examination discovers it to be still there, built into the field bank a few yards away, to the right of the painting, and well covered by tree roots. Carn Ingli can be seen to the West in the distance.

The 48 inch high stump left standing clearly shows the 6 inch hole drilled to break it up, and the ensuing cracks. This must have been a considerable task as it appears to be blue stone and very hard. The thought occurs that the Stone Killers, as Stukeley called them at Avebury, may have had second thoughts about the destruction. They left the stump standing by the field gate and built the broken piece into the hedge. Perhaps they were told that bad luck would befall them if they removed the fields' remaining stone totally.

The remains of an ancient sunken track adjoin the field, and not far away on the main road is the name Post Gwyn (*white post*), where it may be supposed another stone once stood. The word post seems to be used in Pembrokeshire to mean a stone pillar. Not far away are the recurring gate names of Temple Gate, Iet Sais (*Englishman's gate*) and Iet Wen (*white gate*).

FISHGUARD SOUTH PARISH (6)

Ty'n Meini, Dinas Cross

(SM 996 376) NPRN 305 160

One of the best known and most frequently seen monoliths in Pembrokeshire, The Lady Stone, stands white and cone shaped in a field beside the road at a place called Iet-y-Bont-Bren (*wooden bridge gate*). It is approximately 102 inches above ground with a circumference of 114 inches at the five sided base. On the south profile are a series of bumps, and a small characteristic 'nose' three quarters of the way down.

The name of the farm could be translated as ten stones, so it is likely that this is the solitary survivor of a circle or alignment moved many years ago.

The Royal Commission survey states that passengers in horsedrawn coaches would remove their hats and salute the stone when passing; thereby showing the survival of the ancient custom of venerating standing stones. This one was obviously much respected and said to be called The Lady Stone as it resembled a veiled woman; however it is more likely that it was regarded as a female object of worship; or the place, a gate, was another haunt of the phantom, white, fairy being, Ladi Wen.

HAROLDSTON WEST PARISH (7)

St Catherines, Haroldston, Broad Haven (SM 862 147) NPRN 305 339

Standing in a garden on a cliff overlooking St Bride's Bay is one of Pembrokeshire's most interesting and well loved stones.

The Royal Commission survey gave its height as 74 inches, and now though it only measures 66 inches above ground its proportions and interest are still vast. Down each of its sides run various 'V' shaped grooves which cannot be ascribed to natural formation or weathering. Those on the south side are beautifully fan-shaped and terminate just above ground level in a nose-like bulge. Below this are more 'V' shaped grooves running into the ground. The top is flat and wide, its four sides varying in width from 18 to 24 inches. The whole stone sparkles with quartz and it has reputed healing properties.

In general shape it is rather like the Ffynnondruidion stone but in much better preserve in spite of its exposed position and shaggy grey lichen-covered surface. Similar grooves can be noticed on other stones such as the one at Brynawel, Newport, and Sandy Haven Farm, though those on the latter are less obvious because of the weathering of the sandstone.

Richard Fenton described in his *Historical Tour* through Pembrokeshire how he searched the surface of the Haroldstone for an inscription which Giraldus stated Harold had cut on various *meini hirion* to commemorate his victories. He eventually concluded this stone was much older than that period of history.

One hundred yards to the south are the Upper Lodge Stones, which, because they are incorporated in a road bank are barely visible and a satisfactory painting would be difficult. Apparently they were originally part of a circle which was moved.

HAYSCASTLE PARISH (8)

Rhyndaston Fawr, Hayscastle

(SM 896 224) NPRN 305 325

This appears to be a very interesting area where many roads, paths and field boundaries radiate in a star-shape from a central point. Not far away is the splendid *maen hir* standing more than 84 inches high. It is almost triangular in plan with two wide sides, narrowed back and chair-shaped front. The wedge-shaped top is notched.

Nearby are the ruined remains of a tumulus where fine Bronze Age urns were found in the last century and there are other ancient sites in the locality. Tumuli and cairns can be seen on the hills; lightening flashed round them and thunder rumbled menacingly whilst I painted.

Jill Young

HENRY'S MOAT PARISH (9)

Budloy Stone, Goetty Uchaf, Rosebush

(SN 065 285) NPRN 304 449

The field called Parc-maen-hir (*long stone field*), in which this striking pillar of stone stands, now belongs to Goetty Uchaf Farm.

The sides of the stone at the bottom measure roughly 24 inches each, and its height above ground is 102 inches. At its base is a piece of stone which appears to have been broken from the top, so with this addition the total height would have been 132 inches. It does not stand securely in the ground and has fallen and been re-erected. Nearby is the Dyffryn Cairn circle, and other stones which may have been the remains of a cromlech with which this standing stone was associated.

It has been said that this monolith showed signs of having been worked with a tool on the side which faces the circle. However there appears to be less evidence of this stone having been worked than many others examined in the course of the present exercise.

HUBBERSTON PARISH (10)

Dale Bay Farms Ltd, St Botolph's Mansion, Hubberston (SN 892 071) NPRN 305 351

The long stone on Lodge Farm is not strictly a standing stone. It appears to be the remaining central part of a burial chamber. It was included in the collection because of its beautiful shape and the colour of the red sandstone; and since the area seems to be almost completely covered in oil storage tanks with little of the past history and beauty left undisturbed.

Jill Young

JORDANSTON PARISH (11)

Rhos-y-Clegyrn 11, Clegyrn, Letterston

(SM 916 356) NPRN 305 175

On a different farm and parish, but in the same wet valley only a few hundred yards to the north-east of the Rhos-y-Clegyrn stone where excavations took place between 1962 and 1968, stands another much smaller anvil-shaped stone. The area is surrounded by rocky outcrops on all sides; Goodwick and the sea can be seen to the north east, and more to the East Garn Fawr and the Preseli beyond. The place abounds in huge stones where they lie in the fields and are built into the hedge banks. Since Fenton explored this area it is evident that many stones of interest have been removed to make field enclosures, so that the sites of the antiquities he mentioned can only be surmised.

The valley with its magical quality is one of extreme interest and it may not be difficult to find the remains of the habitation where the people lived who erected and used the stones as part of their cultural practise.

It may be possible to discover domestic items and excavation of such a site of human habitation rather than one of worship may reveal information about the people without disturbing their strategically placed stones. The stones seem to lose their power when removed.

The anvil-shaped stone is 46 inches high with a flat triangular top. The back is more or less flat and the front tapers to a few inches at the top of the 'nose'. In the past it has fallen and been re-erected.

LLANFAIR-NANT-Y-GOF PARISH (12)

Llygadcleddau, nr Tre-cŵn

(SM 981 336) NPRN 305 192

A spectacular view of St Bride's Bay, Wolfscastle, Garn Fawr, and the coast to the north can be seen from the slopes of the hill where the stone stands. The Irish mountains and Snowdon show clearly in certain weather conditions from the farm house just below. Until reclamation, the slopes were covered in heather and boulders; traces of a circular earth-work 150ft in diameter, were noted in the Royal Commission survey in the field called Parc-y-Castell (*castle field*) above Parc Carreg (*stone field*) where the stone stands. An ancient track passes over the hill and runs towards the Trellwyn Fawr alignment.

The brownish stone is roughly triangular in plan, though five-sided, and is of the pillar type. It stands 73 inches above ground but appears to have been shortened in the past; it is beautifully shaped and many faceted.

So many *meini hirion* have been 'fired' and broken in past centuries for various reasons, and groups removed except for one, in the belief that one stone must be left, perhaps as a peace offering. This may have been one of a pair. It has been noticed that the narrower partners of pairs are often triangular in plan.

There are stones in the hedges with the same marks upon them as can be seen near Bedd Morys and Gors Fawr. It is difficult to judge their age and no information has been found about them. They seem to occur on stones by road sides or sites of now unused tracks. They could have been made by surveyors, tramps or perhaps drovers who were incidentally notorious for taking chips from stones for good luck.

Gill Young

LLANFYRNACH PARISH (13)

Maen Gwyn Hir, Bryn Meini, Llanfyrnach

(SN 239 302) NPRN 275 685

Since the Royal Commission survey one of this pair of splendid stones has been removed, and no doubt the remaining one owes its survival to the fact that the roadside bank and hedge have been built up to it. They must have been a most impressive pair; the existing one was 134 inches high, and the one which was disappeared was 96 inches above the soil. Opinions differ as to its exact position. Such vandalism is pointless as so little inconvenience would have been caused by this stone, and little land lost.

The solitary partner is most interestingly shaped with its notched and pointed top descending in an angular protuberance before becoming undercut at another angle from whence it sweeps elegantly downwards into the ground. The front swells to a human-like shape, similar to that of the stone at Trefelgarn Farm, St Nicholas. Great care should be taken of this monolith as there are dangerous looking cracks in it.

Before this land was enclosed in the 18th century, according to Lewis' Topographical Dictionary, it was possible to see from a great distance four large stones on the common above the church. It was thought then that they marked the graves of two great chieftains who were killed there in a desperate battle. No doubt two were this pair and the others were on the neighbouring farm Nant-y-Groes, but it is doubtful that they were erected as grave markers.

LLANFYRNACH PARISH (14)

SSW of Moor Farm, Nant-y-Groes, Llanfyrnach (SN 208 312) NPRN 304 108

It is said that the companion to this huge erect slab was buried somewhere when it was removed to facilitate ploughing. Here again the idea recurs that moving was legitimate if one stone was left standing. Refreshingly different from his predecessors the present Keeper of the stone would like to find and re-erect the missing partner. This would of course also mean finding not only the monolith but also the original site, now both lost for many years, and the exact position of the stone. It would not be impossible for a competent dowser. Apparently it stood 6 feet 6 inches high above ground; doubtless this pair, with the pair at Bryn Meini made up the four which could be seen from afar on the common above the church. It is interesting to note the growth of vegetation since the enclosures; these two remaining stones, widowed as might be said of their partners, are now separated by an impenetrable boundary hedge.

This monolith comes into the category of slab shapes, with wide sides and narrower back and front. The back is flat, the top is straight and then slopes down to a 'nose' on the narrow front.

The giant stone stands proudly 108 inches above the clover and clouds of pinky fescue. Round the base there were 'offerings', a circle of small quartz stones.

Jill Young

LLANFYRNACH PARISH (15)

Rhyd-y-Gath, Llanfyrnach (SN 212 311) NPRN 304 109

This attractively shaped stone stands in a field called Parc-y-Maen on sloping ground, to the south east and below the Nant-y-Groes stone, on a different farm.

The top is 78 inches above ground and the stone has four sides, one of which has been pointed into two facets at the base. Thus in plan it is similar to Trefais *maen hir*. There are many interesting shapes in this stone, with its sharply pointed top, furrows and protuberances. On one side there are three petal shaped indentations in the form of three arms of a cross.

In the farmyard there is a pointed stone of similar proportions, on the side of which is a small indented circle with a cross in the centre. The cross has a long tail with a curved end. This has every appearance of being a Christianised standing stone and was 'found' in 1937.

There is a mention in the Royal Commission of the Tre Hywel Ogam stone which once stood on a hill called Mynydd Stamba on the farm of Iet Wen in the same parish. It was taken to Glandwr churchyard. On it is carved a similar cross and also an Ogam inscription, but it seems probable that it too was originally a standing stone that had been erected centuries before the birth of Christ.

The name Iet Wen meaning *White Gate* has further interest as there is again the connection of the two words with stones. Also this particular stone was said to have been used as a gate post, so there might have been a pair, not for holding a gate, but for making a way through, to timelessness, perhaps. The Gors Fawr Circle legend of running round the circle before passing through the two stones, may apply to other pairs.

LLANGOLMAN PARISH (16)

Maen y Parc, Glynsaithmaen, Mynachlog Ddu (SN 111 303) NPRN 304 064

In typical mountain sheep country with grass bitten like a lawn and ground iron hard, this tall monolith seems to be about to take a step forward. It stands on ground rising to Foel Cwmcerwyn, and on the horizon are the notch of Tafarn-y-Bwlch and the summit of Carn Ingli.

This pinkish stone, beautifully encrusted with green and gold lichens is 90 inches tall. It has four sides and is of the pillar type. The top is chisel-shaped, and the silhouette seems to be divided into several more or less equal parts by bumps or indentations like those noticed on some other stones.

The proximity of the farm called Gate enhances the idea that there may have been a pair of stones here or nearby, and the names of hills in the vicinity suggest the possibility of a terrestial zodiac similar to that suggested at Glastonbury. This Preseli country also has many Arthurian legends and the existence of at least one zodiac has been claimed in Wales.

In the valley below, the stone is in its Keeper's farm Glynsaithmaen (*valley of seven stones*), an ancient place of habitation where huge stones lie about in the yard under tall trees. At one time six other stones could be seen from a *maen hir* which stood there. Field names indicate that others stood in them. A monolith with chisel marks on it was said to have been situated by the bridge two hundred yards away from the farm.

The name Seven Stones occurs at other places in Wales. It has been suggested that the farm's name could be derived from Saethau, meaning arrows which were said to have been dedicated on stones of particular sanctity.

Jill Young

LLANLLAWER PARISH (17)

Trellwyn Fawr Farm, Llanllawer (SM 998 359) NPRN 285

A field bank is built around and between this splendid Parc-y-Meirw alignment of eight monoliths. Now only four are clearly visible as the others are almost concealed in the bank. Two serve as gate posts, one of which has been much chipped by souvenir hunters to reveal the blue stone beneath the lichen-covered surface. At least one stone has ancient marks upon it when seen in certain lights.

A detailed description of this well known site was published in Archaeologica Cambrensis 1868, and included a reproduction of drawings made by J. T. Blight two years previously. Parc y Meirw (*field of the dead*) behind the stones was described as a place of ancient interest; and of the legend of yet another ghostly white lady who haunted it. The chance of seeing this apparition so frightened the local people they made a detour of nearly a mile to avoid the place at night. There was also a local tradition of a battle fought among the stones.

Two 19th century clergymen described the ruination of a cromlech. The culprit, who was told bad luck would overtake those who destroyed Druids' altars, later admitted that the house he had built with the stone had proved unlucky.

In 1967 Professor A. Thom mentioned this alignment of stones in his book *Megalithic Sites in Britain*; the report of his painstaking surveys of over 600 sites. He connected their geometrical and astronomical features and those of outlying stones with rising and setting points of the sun at solstices, and also the moon and stars, in the creation of calendars. He found that they were laid out with the greatest accuracy by people with a sophisticated knowledge of geometry, using a measurement of 2.72 feet which he termed the Megalithic Yard.

He made a plea for every stone to be left untouched where it lies until a meticulate survey has been carried out. This entreaty can be taken further, as even when these surveys have been completed, we must wait until the exact purpose of the stones has been discovered before moving them.

LLANWNDA PARISH (18)

Ladies Gate, Glas Fryn, Llanwnda

(SN 908 392) NPRN 305 171

Standing alone in sunburnt grass in a field called Parc Hen (*old field*), on the rocky windswept headland, this stone seems small at first sight; as a neighbour said, *'There is no top to it.'* It is however, a considerable block, square in section, each side measuring approximately 48 inches across. It now stands 66 inches above ground though at the period of the Royal Commission survey it measured 80 inches. It has obviously sunk or been truncated since then, and the shape of the sides give the appearance of there having been more at the top than at present. It still has great atmosphere and scale.

A short distance away is the Carn Wnda cromlech, three more on Garn Wen, and others on Garngilfach.

This wild promontory has been little disturbed through the centuries and has the remains of many megalithic monuments. Not far from here in 1797, three French ships landed troops in an attempt at an invasion.

LLANWNDA PARISH (19)

Parc Hen Stone, Gilfach Farm, Goodwick (SN 908 392) NPRN 305 171

Had it not been for recent gorse burning it would have been difficult to find this fallen giant, where it lay in its own hollow surrounded by bluebells, ferns and young bracken curls. It is a four-sided stone, and 102 inches of its length can be measured, little of it being beneath the soil now. The rare opportunity arises of being able to examine the top surface.

The fall must have occurred many years ago yet the stone is grand even in its reclining position. Richard Fenton's account of his excavations there in his Historical Tour through Pembrokeshire published in 1811 may provide the reason for the stone's collapse. He wrote of *'two remarkable meini hirion, about three hundred yards from each other, erected probably to commemorate a battle fought between the natives and the invaders, as from this spot a well pitched military road may be traced up to the camp. The gate on the high road leading between the above rude columns is called the Lady's Gate, from a belief prevailing among the common people there, that a treasure is hid near, and that a lady is often seen by night hovering round as if in wait for the happy person who is fated to be enriched by her discovery of the mysterious and valuable deposit.*

In order, if possible to ascertain the intention of raising those stones I dug deeply round one of them, but found nothing that could in any way tend to throw a light on their mystery.'

The legend of the lady in connection with stones, gates and wells occurs often. Note the similarity in the name Lady's Gate and the Lady Stone near Iet-y-Bont-Bren which may connect the places with the phantom white fairy being of ancient mythology; she was identified with Gwenhwyfar, Arthur's queen, and the White Lady of the Sword and the White Lady of the Lake.

No trace could be found of the second stone of this pair.

Jill Young

MAENCLOCHOG PARISH (20)

Parc y Tywod, Galchen Farm, Maenclochog (SN 088 278) NPRN 304 453

Since the Royal Commission survey this *maen hir* has either sunk or been shortened over 12 inches, though its pointed top does not show signs of recent damage. It now measures 88 inches high above ground level and is roughly 24 inches square at the base. It stands in a paddock named Parc-y-Tywod (*sand field*); as its base are some smaller stones and a slab, and in the field walls are many other well shaped stones.

In the past there were many more megalithic monuments in the district which have since been removed. Fenton related the clearance of the cromlech at Temple Druid which took place before his visit. Many huge stones lie near the roadside in the vicinity of that house.

MAENCLOCHOG PARISH (21)

Cornel Bach Pair, Tŷ Newydd, Maenclochog (SN 082 279) NPRN 304 454

These two stones of sharply contrasting shapes are over forty-five yards apart, thus differing from other pairs, but their shapes are so complimentary it has been thought correct to include them as such. At first sight the larger of the two is almost ball shaped, and the other is pyramidical. Both are roughly four sided and taper towards the top; they measure 60 inches and 66 inches in height. The shorter broader stone has many facets and a saddle-like ridge on its top. The other is sharp and chisel-shaped.

They stand on ground which slopes slightly towards a tributary of the Eastern Cleddau and are known as the Cornel Bach pair, taking their name for some reason from the cottages across the main Fishguard Road.

Over the field hedge there are remnants of other large stones which, in view of the terrible destruction of megalithic monuments which took place in this district in past centuries, may be remains of other standing stones.

Richard Fenton tells of the village receiving its name 'Mânclochog-Ringing Stone', *'from two large stones that lay near the roadside, about a bowshot from the church, possessing that property, now broken and removed, but perfect and held in great veneration in Edward Llhwyd's time'*. This refers to the late 17th century.

Jill Young

MATHRY PARISH (22)

Tynewyddgrug, Wolfscastle

(SM 925 287) NPRN 305 214

At the date of the Royal Commission survey this wonderful stone stood 105 inches above ground. It is now twelve inches shorter, has four sides and the front is sliced steeply upwards to a point at the top. It is composed of the most beautiful conglomerate of pink and white quartz with reddish purple Caerfai type pebbles embedded in it. When it was newly erected it must have shone and glistened in the sunlight in a wonderful manner. Now grey and yellow lichens grow on the surface so the colouring is brilliant.

Round the stone the surface of the field is littered with fragments of the same quartz which may be pieces chipped from this stone by vandals and souvenir hunters, or perhaps they are the remnants of another stone which stood nearby.

There does not appear to be any of this type of rock in the vicinity so it may have been transported for some distance.

Twenty yards away from the monolith are the remains of a tumulus with which it may have been associated, but this was destroyed in 1890 when the stones from the middle were used in the buildings of the farm. Two pots were found when the mound was opened, one with stripes round it, and a smaller one. Both were destroyed. The field is named Parc y Garreg.

MYNACHLOG-DDU PARISH (23)

Cerrig Meibion Arthur, Cwm Garw, Mynachlog-ddu (SN 118 310) NPRN 304 065

This must be the most dramatic pair of monoliths in Pembrokeshire, sentinels of their lonely, boggy, stoney valley surrounded on nearly all sides by wild hill tops crowned with carneddau and tumuli. The Afon Wern, tributary of the Eastern Cleddau flows brown in its rocky bed past the old farmhouse surrounded with laburnums, and near the standing stones. Mountain sheep and ponies close-graze the grass amongst boulders, rushes and gorse.

As in other pairs, these stones seem to compliment each other; one is sturdy and massive, the other elegantly needle-shaped.

The slim stone is not quite as tall and is leaning. Near the more massive of the two is another long stone, prostrate in the grass with only a small portion visible above ground. It is possible there may have been an alignment here, and many large stones lie on the ground in the vicinity.

The area in which these stones stand is near Glynsaithmaen, Dolau Maen where there is another pair, and the Gors Fawr Circle and Pair. It is connected with the story in the *Mabinogion* in which four of Arthur's companions were killed by the Twrch Trwyth (the mythological pig) and *'he himself was wounded in Cwm Cerwyn'*. Foel Cwmcerwyn is the name of the highest hill to the West of the valley. An ancient track runs along the top of these hills to end eventually at the coast.

The name of Arthur is perpetuated in the district in Carn Arthur and Bedd Arthur (*Arthur's grave*); the idea of the zodiac occurs again, and the area is full of ancient mystery and magical romanticism.

Jill Young

MYNACHLOG-DDU PARISH (24)

Waun Llwyd, Dolaumaen, Mynachlog-ddu

(SN 158 312) NPRN 304 054

A pair of magnificent stones stand over 24 feet apart in a pasture known as Gweirglodd-y-Maen which slopes down to the infant Cleddau. The ground rises steeply to high hills on either side of the valley. Sheep graze round the stones and laburnum grows in the hedges. This must have been a particularly important site to Neolithic Man as from the vicinity of Carn Menyn on the hills to the north west the famous blue stones of Stonehenge were said to have been quarried. The air was heavy with the scent of may blossom and the sky with thunder; lightning flashed round the tumuli on the hill tops while the painting was done, but sheep quietly grazed the lush grass between the brilliant rushes.

The name of the farm is spelt Dolau Main or Maen, (*main* being a plural version of *maen*). There are in the district three other farms with stones names, Carnmeini Uchaf, Ganol and Isaf (*upper, middle and lower stones cairn*). Is it too fanciful to suggest that the magical blue stones began their journey to Salisbury Plain by being pushed and floated along the little river that flows past these farms?

As in the case of the Cerrig Meibion Arthur pair, one of these stones is thin and the other more massive. The thin one is 90 inches tall.

The more massive stone is also 90 inches high. This stone slopes slightly. The Royal Commission survey noted two other prostrate stones in the same field in line with the standing stones and suggests an alignment. Significantly the next field is named Parc-y-Maen and could have had a stone in it also to continue the alignment.

MYNACHLOG-DDU PARISH (25)

Gors Fawr Standing Stones and Circle, Mynachlog-ddu (SN 135 295) NPRN 304 281

Professor A Thom included Gors Fawr in his survey, and noted a circle, two menhirs, and a long alignment. Seventy two feet across, the circle is composed of sixteen small stones about four and a half yards apart, most of which are less than 36 inches high. They are in fact so small it is not difficult to realise the ease with which many similar sites must have been destroyed. It is also possible that some sites are yet uncharted and are being destroyed in modern times.

The outlying standing stones are roughly one hundred and fifty yards to the north east of the circle; they are undoubtedly important.

In the vicinity of the stones are many banks and undulations in the unploughed common land, and many large and small stones. It is possible that in this area were many earthworks and standing stone patterns marking a place of particular sanctity.

In recent years part of the roadside boundary bank has been removed, replaced by a wire fence and kissing gate, and the stones and debris dumped on the common. Dowser Tom Graves made interesting discoveries when working at Gors Fawr concerning stored energy released by the destruction of the roadside bank; he gave warning of the serious problems which can arise when such sites are disturbed.

Guy Underwood mentions the importance of huge stone field gateposts as links between major and minor sacred sites, thus being markers of processional routes. This could explain the experiences of Tom Graves at the ruined henge at Gors Fawr, and also point to the inadvisability of moving old gate posts, however inconvenient.

Locally the only name for the standing stones is the two posts by Traethllwyn, the farm beside the common. The grandmother of a neighbouring farmer remembered a ritual which took place there in her youth. The children understood that they must run in and out of alternate stones of the circle before they could pass between the pair of stones. It was not remembered how many times this should be done, nor at what time of year, but the practice has definite similarities with those which took place at other ancient circles and single stones, and children's games. Even beating parish boundaries which are usually marked with stones, or maypole dancing where they 'threaded the needle', could be associated with this ritual. It seemed to take place at special seasons, or phases of the moon; energetic practices such as running or even crawling round stones, usually with the sun rather than against it may have originated in the idea of necessity to increase, or release, the earth's stored power.

Gill Young

MOYLEGROVE PARISH (26)

Trefais Farm, Moylegrove

(SN 117 429) NPRN 304 098

On this farm is another example of a massive stone which seems to have been truncated in previous centuries, and is now only 60 inches high at its tallest edge; this is much weathered and gives the appearance of having been broken. There is however a considerable amount of the stone below ground. It is basically square in plan, with each side measuring about 36 inches wide, but one of the sides is pointed in a 'nose-shaped front', similar to that of the Haroldston West stone and the Rhos-y-Clegyrn *maen hir*.

It is composed of an interesting conglomerate which seems to incorporate a type of limestone with small pieces of quartz and blue stone.

The Trefais stone and the Trellyffaint *maen hir* are the only two authenticated standing stones near this part of the coast, though there was once one (or more to judge by the farm's name) at Blaenmeini (*head valley stones*); a cup-marked stone said to be at Bayvil is thought to have been part of a burial chamber. Many remains of the latter type of megalithic monument are to be found in the district; one explanation for their survival is the difficulty of moving them. Monoliths were relatively easy to drag into hedge banks for building, or use as gate posts.

NEVERN PARISH (27)

Brynawel, Newport

(SN 091 354) NPRN 413 138

The undulating ridge of the Preseli makes a wild and beautiful background to the 78 inches high stone where it stands near farm buildings named Pen Parke. It is basically triangular in shape, with sides at the base roughly 36 inches wide, and looks pyramidical at first glance. The silhouette conforms with others when examined, the top is most beautifully pointed, and the facets, parallel grooves and ridges give every appearance of having been purposely made. This may have been one of a pair.

It is an important stone in a district rich in megalithic monuments, the most famous of which is Pentre Ifan cromlech.

Jill Young

NEVERN PARISH (28)

Parc Lan Pair, Cilgwyn, Newport

(SN 090 358) NPRN 304 325

This most interesting pair of stones are small yet of such scale they might be many times their size. One is slab-shaped, about 10 inches thick and 24-28 inches on the wide sides. It stands 48 inches above ground. The surface of the side opposite Carnedd Meibion Owen has a series of holes similar to those on cupmarked stones, and three vertical grooves, all of which give the impression of having been man-made. The pointed top has a notch positively cut in the centre of it. One's immediate reaction when seeing this, is to take a sighting through it to the other stone which reveals the undulations of the hills on the horizon.

The other stone is of a tall narrow shape, 63 inches high, and of basically triangular section, with sides roughly 24 inches wide. The top is chisel-shaped and the silhouette has similarities with some others.

Quartz in the stones glistens in the sunlight; they are covered with rough lichens, and the droppings of perching birds emphasise the irregularities on their surfaces.

This splendid pair was said to have been moved, but they are most assuredly standing on the hillside, guarding their secret still in the field known as Parc Lan.

NEVERN PARISH (29)

Y Garreg Hir, Gelli Fawr, Newport

(SN 039 392) NPRN 304 345

Dominating the lower slopes of Banc Du on which it stands above Cwm Gwaun, and the countless boulders lying in the bracken and grass, this huge stone stands 96 inches high above ground. Its four sides each measure approximately 36 inches at shoulder height. Its bulging front, flat back and pointed top have similar proportions and silhouette to stones at Bryn Meini, Puncheston, Trefelgarn, etc. The lowest part of the stone is reddish coloured, characteristic of many stones, and the top has grey, black, gold and green lichens upon it.

Much stone clearing has taken place here in recent years, but there seems to be a rough circle of small boulders round the *maen hir*.

The Royal Commission report measured it as being 108 inches high, and remarked on five large stones fifteen yards away to the West, surmising they may have been part of a cromlech.

NEVERN PARISH (30)

Waun Mawn Common Stone, Nevern

(SN 084 340) NPRN 300 423

The vast *maen hir* shines silvery amongst the surrounding stones and heather in this magical place, and can be seen from a distance. 88 inches of it show above ground and the widest of the four sides measures 45 inches. The stone is narrow at the base, then three of the four sides bulge out before tapering up to the pointed, notched top. It has a flat fourth side from top to bottom, like many other monoliths. Similarities in the shaping can be noticed at Fagwyr y Frân, Rhos-y-Clegyrn, Cerrig Meibion Arthur and others.

The circular hollow in which the stone stands fills with water. The surrounding grass is brilliantly green amongst the heather and close-bitten pasture.

It is situated just to the north of the farm road leading to Gernos-Fach, and is on the same privately owned common.

NEVERN PARISH (31)

Waun Mawn Common Stones, Nevern

(SN 080 339) NPRN 304 355

On a level area of land on the south facing slope of Waun Mawn is a mysterious group which appear to be the remains of an oval of stones. They are not authenticated as standing stones and though the only one left erect does not strictly come into the category, the site was irresistible, and so has been included in the collection.

The report in the Royal Commission seems fairly accurate though it is felt that a circle rather than an oval was being considered.

The one stone left standing is 60 inches above ground, and is beautifully shaped. It is flanked by two fallen monoliths 132 inches and 144 inches long. The tips of two more can be discovered in the same arc, and there are others below ground. Considering the stones at Callanish in the Outer Hebrides were half covered in peat before they were excavated in the last century it is not unlikely that some of these on Waun Mawn are also below the surface. Everywhere there are peat, pockets of clay, streams bubbling out of the hillside, and bogs.

In Spring, after heather burning, outside the perimeter of the 'oval' on the south-western side can be seen above ground the tips of several stones which seem to be connected with the others – as if an entrance.

On Cnwc-yr-Hydd, the summit of Waun Mawn, is a ruinous area which might if excavated reveal a burial place; and on the north-western side the dwelling places of the people whose culture may have involved the use of the stones.

Jill Young

NEVERN PARISH (32)

Tafarn-y-Bwlch Common, Nevern

(SN 081 332) NPRN 413 139

In the abundance of huge rocks which line the road, and hillsides of Foel Eryr and Waun-Maes to Tafarn-y-Bwlch it is not difficult to miss the wedge-shaped stone standing on the verge amongst the heather. As much of it may be buried, it is probably more massive than its height of 74 inches. The two widest sides above ground measure 50 inches and there are two narrower sides sloping up to the slim top in which there is a notch. To the north west in the valley the stone pair is clearly visible. This stone seems to point the way to others half way up Cnwc-yr-Hydd. Half buried in the turf and heather are other stones which may be part of a cist and to do with the standing stone.

Near here part of a mountain track, running from a ford and the tumulus on the far side of Rhwngyddwyffordd, joins the road, and its line can be seen as it ascends the opposite hill of Cnwc-yr-Hydd to the stones there.

This land is privately owned common, is grazed by various farmers' livestock, and visitors should treat it with due respect for its unique character.

NEVERN PARISH (33)

Tafarn-y-Bwlch Pair, Nevern

(SN 082 337) NPRN 304 356

These beautiful stones stand only about 48 inches high above ground level, though it is possible they may have sunk in the wet peaty soil. They are 45 inches apart and are closer together than most, but they are generally accepted as a pair.

The top of the more massive stone is flattish and slightly domed; the four sides slope inwards to the narrow top.

The other stone is similar in width on two sides, but is only a few inches thick. The top is wedge-shaped, narrowing to a thin chisel-like sloping edge. The lower part of one thin side swells out in a bulging silhouette. This stone is leaning badly and looks in danger of falling, as do members of the pairs at Dolau Maen and Cerrig Meibion Arthur. The hollow in which the pair stand is rushy and fills with water in wet weather.

Though so small these stones can be seen clearly from a distance, and from their neighbouring single stones on the main road, and the farm road to Gernos Fach, and the group of stones on Waun Mawn. This is beautiful, atmospheric country, wild and heather covered, grazed by mountain sheep and ponies, and little touched by man for centuries.

JM Young

NEVERN PARISH (34)

Trellyffaint, Newport

(SN 083 423) NPRN 304 397

Three hundred yards to the south east of the fine Trellyffaint burial chamber are the rather chair-shaped remains of what must once have been a fine monolith. At the time of the Royal Commission survey it measured 54 inches but is now 12 inches shorter. The desecration must have taken place several centuries ago because the stump is much weathered. From the width of the four sides at ground level it can be deduced that the height could have been at least 96 inches No doubt it suffered from the same fanatic firing as did so many others.

The cromlech is notable for the fact that its capstone is ornamented with cupmarks, mysterious circular carvings, rarely recorded in Wales. Fenton visited this ancient homestead but made no mention of the cromlech and standing stone. Instead he quoted Giraldus Cambrensis' curious story of Syssilt Longshanks who was eaten up by toads. Fenton saw a toad carved in black marble fixed in the chimney piece and covered by glass for protection. It was said to have been sent from Italy by Sir Richard Macon, Knight of the Green Cloth to James II to his relatives at Trellyffaint who *'bore a toad for their crest'*. It was last heard of in the house of Morris Owen Esq in Haverfordwest whose arms were a 'toad proper'. Fenton noted that the owners of the farm in his day were all remarkably tall but did not know whether they were descended from the victim of the *'horrid visitation'*.

The present owners have no connection with this family.

NEWPORT PARISH (35)

Carn Ingli Common, Newport

(SN 038 365) NPRN 276 042

The road from Newport to Pontfaen crosses wild, heather covered hill country. At the highest point and on the side of the road, for all travellers to see, stands a beautifully shaped *maen hir*. Many pass by, but few people realise its importance. It has not escaped the notice of modern man, for on it are cut various inscriptions, to say nothing of the scars from which samples and momentos have been taken recently, as well as in past centuries.

This elegant stone stands over 84 inches above ground, with one side bowed out in a beautiful curve, and a sloping chisel-shaped top. On its north-western side are marks similar to those on the stone at Fagwyr-frân, and near the base are several stones with the appearance of having been cut with marks similar to those at Llygadcleddau, Gelli-Fawr and Gors-Fawr and others. It points along a straight part of the road directly in line with the cairns on Mynydd Cilciffeth.

The legend of the name does not point to the origin of the stone but comes from an old story of a robber known as Morris, Morys, or Maurice, who lived in the rocks nearby. There may be some sort of burial beneath the stone but not of this man, who would no doubt have met with his end on the gallows at the junction of this road and the present main road from Dinas to Newport.

(This wonderful stone has been vandalised recently (2012), toppled and broken. It is to be repaired but can never be the same again.)

Jill Young

NEWPORT PARISH (36)

Y Garreg Hir, Hendre, Newport

(SN 064 351) NPRN 304 309

This stone, known as Y Garreg Hir, *The Long Stone*, was particularly elusive, but when discovered proved to be a sturdy 60 inch high monolith with sides 54 inches wide, and pointed ends. It is composed of blue spotted dolerite and sparkles with crystals in places. The surface has been smoothed by centuries of weathering and is beautifully coloured blue/grey and pink. The interesting facets and sinister eye-like hole give the impression of it having been purposely shaped, and the silhouette is similar to that of other standing stones.

The position is in an area of great beauty with the sea on one side and a steep escarpment topped with rocks and cairns on the other.

A stream runs overground from the hills, through Hendre Farm, where it once worked a mill, then under the road, and along the side of the field called Parc Garreg Hir (*long stone field*) where the stone stands near part of an ancient and overgrown coastal road.

PUNCHESTON PARISH (37)

No 7 Council Houses, Puncheston

(SN 006 298) NPRN 304 466

Of all the places in Pembrokeshire in which standing stones are to be found this is perhaps the most unusual. That this, surely one of the most spectacular stones in the county, was not removed when the chapel was built nearby is surprising. Perhaps it was covered in bushes at the time. The builders of the present houses had thoughts about removing it, but fortunately it was left to dominate the small garden where it still stands.

It is a gigantic monolith standing 108 inches above the garden soil, with a flat back, grand broad sides and a sloping top, altogether sculptural. Its general shape and prominences have similarities to stones at Fagwyr y Frân, Cerrig Meibion Arthur, Bryn Meini and others. Markings on this stone are significantly similar to those on others, and it does not seem sensible to dismiss them as having been caused by weathering. The 'decorations' on one corner in particular are very similar to those on the narrow stone at Dolau Maen, and the pairs of holes appear fairly frequently.

This stone has apparently sunk 12 inches since the date of the Royal Commission survey.

PUNCHESTON PARISH (38)

Carreg Coetan Arthur, Church Farm, Puncheston (SN 009 302) NPRN 304 361

A thick blackthorn hedge almost hides this splendid *maen hir*; however it is possible that its survival is due to the field bank being built up to it. Measurements are difficult to take but its height appears to be between 84 and 96 inches. The side opposite Mynydd Castlebythe is flat and wonderfully coloured with brilliant red and yellow lichen. The stone at the base may have connections with the monolith. The name Carreg Coetan (*quoit stone*) implies that there was once a legend that the stone was hurled like a quoit from a distance by a mysterious being; this is a story which occurs frequently in connection with stones in folk lore.

PUNCHESTON PARISH (39)

Fagwyr y Frân West Farm, Puncheston

(SN 005 315) NPRN 304 362

The ground slopes up to the mountains except on one side in the direction of Wolfscastle whose craggy silhouette can be seen in the distance. There is a feeling of age and open spaces when looking past the stone to the heather covered slopes of Mynydd Castlebythe.

This stone bears a resemblance in shape and proportion to many others. The chisel-shaped top, flat face, prominences and indentations are at similar heights. The facets of one side are particularly like those of Bedd Morys. It is 94 inches tall, leaning rather dangerously, slender in proportion, roughly triangular in plan but with corners cut off, and of the pillar type. It may have been connected with a line of small boulders which were in the adjoining field.

Like many standing stones it has an attraction for animals and their tracks can be seen leading to and from it.

ST DAVID'S PARISH (40)

Maen Dewi, Drws Gobaith, St David's

(SM 775 275) NPRN 305 373

The historians Jones and Freeman were unable to find this vast monolith as it had been built into the end of a *tŷ unnos*, a dwelling erected hurriedly overnight on common land. The remains of this cottage are still to be seen in the garden of the present house, but the major portion of the stone is now uncovered. The front narrow face appears to have been cut out as a key for building. The ruins are covered in the pink spikes and shiny leaves of pennywort, and the vast stone is spotted with white and yellow lichens on the top, while the base is pink. In the distance is the summit of Pen Berry.

Standing 108 inches high, its widest side is 82 inches broad and its narrowest 30 inches. It is astonishing that it is still as tall as it is because the surrounding land is water-logged and marshy.

This *maen hir* was named Maen Dewi after the patron saint as was one which existed at Whitchurch. Half a mile nearer to St David's is a farm called Maen Dewi which may mean that there was another stone at that place. The name Drws Gobaith (*door of hope*) has been said to mean the end in sight of the pilgrim's journey to the holy shrine at St David's. Alternatively there could be connections with the gate names which occur frequently in places near standing stones.

ST DAVID'S PARISH (41)

Trecenny, St David's

(SM 766 257) NPRN 305 397

Near the edge of a field called Parc Garreg Fawr (*big stone field*) on a sharp bend in the road by Trecenny Farm, this great stone commands a view of St Bride's Bay. It stands nearly 96 inches above ground and has two broad sides and two narrow ones. Tŵr-y-Felin can be seen to the south west.

Some years ago it was struck by lightning and fell, but was re-erected in a concrete base. Here is another example of the old tradition of the difficulty of moving megalithic monuments: the efforts of horses and thirty men were needed to put the monolith back in place. It has obviously been respectfully regarded in the past and was understood by its past Keepers to be one of many way-markers which existed in the days before there were roads, and in line with another stone in the county.

Thunder rolled in the sky while the painting was being done; however this quite common occurrence has also been noticed by other painters of megalithic monuments.

The next field is called Parc-Garreg-Fach (*little stone field*) and the stone that was sadly moved from there was understood to be a rubbing stone.

In 1856 Jones and Freeman recorded another stone, 66 inches high, 48 inches broad and 18 inches thick which must have been one of the slab type stones. It stood a little to the left of the upper road to Fishguard and not far from the Trecenny stone which was then 'reclining'.

Gill Young

ST DOGWELL'S PARISH (42)

Lower Broadmoor, Letterston

(SM 952 277) NPRN 110 339

This is an impressive stone of brownish sedimentary rock and seems to fill the small field in which it stands with its atmosphere. The field is named Gweirglodd y Garreg (*stone meadow*), and lies beside a very old walled road running from the farm in the direction of the river to the north of Wolfscastle. The stone's roughly chisel-shaped top is approximately 102 inches above ground. It has one wide side and three narrower ones with pronounced facets.

ST EDRIN'S PARISH (43)

Trehale Fam, Trehale House, Mathry (Treddiog Farm) (SM 886 288) NPRN 305 311

This old estate, now divided, has at least six stones on it, and at one time there were more. Lists give various OS numbers and the old maps and records show other sites. Since the Royal Commission survey some stones have disappeared or been moved as has the splendid 120 inches long conglomerate monolith now lying beside a hedge on Treddiog Farm. At one time there was another in the same field, named apparently in Welsh, graves. It is a site of interest as there is a record of an oval mound with a slight depression and bank round it. An axe found there is now at Scolton museum. The fallen stone was moved before the present occupier farmed the land, but the depression where it stood could be seen when he moved there.

Two fields away on Trehale Farm is the stump of a stone which shows clear evidence of having been drilled on two sides and blasted, so that it now measures only 45 inches high. It is of the anvil-shaped type.

It seems that drill marks and signs of blasting have caused some surveyors to dismiss old stones as rubbing stones erected in recent centuries.

Another anvil shaped stone is on Trehale Farm, similar to the second one and those at Clegyrn Farm and Tremaenhir. It is four sided, flat topped, 42 inches high, 120 inches in circumference, with a horizontal seam of quartz running through it.

In the paddock near Trehale House stands a fine 70 inches high stone of a laminated quartz conglomerate with a wedge shaped top and four sides.

Two other stones on this important site were not painted. Various landmarks are visible including Rhyndaston, Roch Castle, and St Edrin's Church on an ancient site.

Jill Young

ST ISHMAEL'S PARISH (44)

Sandy Haven House, St Ishmael's

(SM 848 084) NPRN 305 357

In the fairly recent past someone unwisely moved this extremely powerful monolith from its original position. It now stands cracked and leaning drunkenly beside the hedge bank.

It is comprised of plum-coloured laminated sandstone and is covered in brilliantly contrasting pale green and yellow lichens. It now shows 78 inches high above ground and is 42 inches wide by 12 inches thick. It is of the pillar type and similar in shape to one of the stones in the alignment at Trellwyn Fawr, Llanllawer.

Its previous site was found to be about forty yards away from the hedge, and is still very active. After the stone was moved an excavation took place and some cremated remains, 'a handful of powder', and buried stones were uncovered. Pieces of sandstone can be seen on the original site which is dead in line with North Hill on the Angle peninsular, the site of the stone now lost from Skerrybank Farm, Sandy Haven House, and the little cwm behind the stone in the painting.

The Longstone which stood on Skerrybank Farm disappeared without trace before the list in the Pembrokeshire Historian was made in 1966. Sadly, lack of understanding of the importance of monoliths has deprived this district of some of its ancient heritage.

ST ISHMAEL'S PARISH (45)

Mabe's Gate, Trewarren House, St Ishmael's

(SM 828 076) NPRN 305 354

Yellow, black and grey/green lichens cover the surface of the wonderfully plum-coloured laminated sandstone of which this monolith is composed.

There is good reason for calling it the Longstone as it is the tallest in the county and stands 120 inches above the ground. It belongs to the slab type of stone, the sides being 80 inches wide but has a thickness of only 9 to 12 inches. The impression gained is that this *maen hir* has been well respected and cared for through the centuries by its Keepers.

There are no local legends about it but in the neighbouring name of Mabe's Gate, the gate name recurs where there might have been other stones once. The longstone must have been strategically placed as from it can be seen a magnificent view of the coast, with clear views of distant Ramsey Island, Carn Llidi and Pen Berry.

Gill Young

ST NICHOLAS' PARISH (46)

Ffynnon Derwyddon, St Nicholas

(SM 921 365) NPRN 305 181

In wet ground below a ruined hilltop cromlech on the same farm, and in the boggy valley which runs south west through Rhos-y-Clegyrn, stands a beautiful 93 inches tall, four sided monolith.

It is greyish-white with golden and green lichens, and though not as perfect in shape and texture, it is strikingly similar to the Haroldston West *maen hir*. There are the same flat sloping top, fan-like nose-shaped front, and flat back. The next field is known as Parc y Garreg and it is likely another stone stood nearby.

ST NICHOLAS' PARISH (47)

Rhos y Clegyrn, Trefelgarn Farm, St Nicholas (SM 913 355) NPRN 305 175

This beautiful stone is 105 inches high above ground level, and has such grand scale that it appears even taller; it is a perfect sculpture in the landscape. Its four sides are quite narrow at the base, swelling out to a girth of over 144 inches, and the top narrows to a head-like point. The silhouette of the stone appears to be divided into equal parts, and the surface is marked with holes and indentations similar to those on some other stones.

It stands on a wild and draughty moor, full of the atmosphere of the past. Ten yards away are the remains of what has been variously described as a round barrow or an embanked stone circle. The whole area is rich in the remains of a once flourishing civilisation, the most obvious of which are this stone, Ffyst Sampson and Ffynnondruidion burial chambers, the Ffynnondruidion standing stone and the Clegyrn Farm standing stone. Behind the stone in the painting can be seen the craggy summit of Garn Fawr.

A detailed excavation of this Rhos-y-Clegyrn stone and its surroundings was undertaken between the years 1962 and 1968 by J. M. Lewis, M.A., F.S.A. The report, Excavations at 'Rhos-y-Clegyrn Prehistoric Site', St Nicholas, Pembrokeshire, by J. M. Lewis, is published in *Archaeologia Cambrensis* CXXIII 1974.

ST PETROG'S PARISH (48)

Harold Stone, Home Farm, Stackpole

(SR 968 960) NPRN 305 409

Known as the Haroldston or Devil's Quoit this great block of limestone stands beside a hedge adjoining a field track, and upon a small mound of stones. On all sides lie lush woods, the peace of which is destroyed only by intermittent explosions from the MOD firing range.

The stone stands nearly 84 inches high above the surface of the mound, and is 66 inches broad by 16 inches thick. The surface is covered with brilliant white patches and indented all over with circular weathered holes in which snails hide; underneath there is a pinkish glow. Ivy and brambles cover the mound. It could be part of a burial chamber and of a later date than the other two quoits.

Fenton describes it as *'a great flat mass of limestone bedded in an elevated circular mound of stones which merits investigation'*. It is possible it has been 'investigated' as the stone is now 12 inches taller than it was in his day. This difference could be of course due to lowering of the ground level caused by the treading of livestock.

There is some confusion over the identity of this site; the stone in the painting is obviously the same as that which Fenton described. However the Royal Commission survey refers to the removal of the second of the Devil's Quoits to the yard of Stackpole Farm. Perhaps that was yet another stone.

This stone is similar to some of the diamond-shaped stones in the Avebury Circle.

ST PETROG'S PARISH (49)

Devil's Quoit, Sampson Farm, Stackpole (SR 962 963) NPRN 305 410

Commanding a view across a wooded valley this monstrous stone stands half way up a gently sloping bank in an arable field. On the ridge of the hills to the north are the church towers of St Twynnell's and St Petrog's.

The shape of it is similar to that of Maen Dewi but the stone is smaller and now stands 64 inches at its highest point, and 69 inches across. It belongs to the slab type, is oval in plan, the narrow ends measuring roughly 21 inches.

Fenton refers to this as the tallest of the three Devil's Quoits which proves that it is sinking, and there may be as much as four feet buried beneath the soil. The Royal Commission survey measured it as being 78 inches high so the discrepancy in the measurements is probably due to deeper ploughing and soil sliding on the bank. Fenton noted that the stone was *'of singular coloured serpentine'*, and examined it without success as he did others, for an inscription Hic Haroldus Victor Fuit which he hoped to find, believing Harold erected monoliths to mark his victories.

He recounted the folk tale of this and the two other Devil's Quoits which were said to meet annually to dance the hay at Sais' ford before returning to their places.

He also remarked on the monument to a Lady Jane Mansell in St Petrog's church, and the legend which told of her whirling headless round the vicinity in a carriage driven by a headless coachman. Another legend told of her driving a fiery chariot from Tenby which alighted on Sampson farmhouse and crushed it! These fascinating remnants of pre-history in connection with standing stone sites give rise to speculation on the subject of the horse cult and the levitation of stones.

This most beautiful stone is yet another which was found to have been vandalised recently, the newly made scar standing out brightly blue/black against the green and gold lichen-covered surface. In certain lights ancient apparently man-made marks can be seen.

Jill Young

SKOMER PARISH (50)

Harold Stone, Skomer Island

(SM 733 096) NPRN 305 372

Measurements given in the Royal Commission survey indicate a height of 96 inches, but this stone now measures 68 inches above the ground, though it has not been shortened recently.

It seems to be local stone and is very nicely shaped and regular with a wedge shaped top, and sides measuring 24x12x24x18 inches. The upper half leans slightly to the east.

When approaching the island by boat through Jack Sound the stone can be seen clearly on the skyline, guarding the landing place as it has through the centuries. A steep climb up to it reveals the beauty of its lichen covered surface where it stands surrounded by puffin inhabited rabbit holes in the bracken. Sea birds wheel and chatter constantly above, and over the sea below, and voles scamper in the undergrowth. Only one thing mars the pleasure of the visit to this beautiful stone: the discovery of the deplorable habits of hammer-happy stone souvenir hunters. Not content with chopping the coastal rocks they have removed a large sliver from one of the top corners of this very fine monolith exposing the black close-grained interior. However much the surface of standing stones is obscured by lichens, the practice of chipping then is uncouth and destructive.

As the island is no longer grazed it is possible that the usual depression round stones has become filled in, thus explaining the discrepancy between earlier and present measurements of the height of this *maen hir*.

STACKPOLE ELIDOR PARISH (51)

National Trust, Devil's Quoit, Stackpole Warren (SR 983 951) NPRN 305 411

The third Devil's Quoit stands in its flowery wilderness on Stackpole Warren. Surrounded on all sides by the richly wooded parkland of the old estate misty in the distance, this stone was painted in hot still weather. No sound broke the utter stillness, yet the place had a restless atmosphere which so often pervades excavated ancient sites. The sandy soil scratched up by rabbits grew blue clouds of bugloss, red seeded docks and ragwort flitted over by meadow blue butterflies.

The stone is composed of laminated sedimentary rock so has perished and broken, but originally it must have been similar to the Sampson Farm stone. It is slab-shaped and now stands 68 inches high, is 64 inches wide, oval in plan, with 12 inch thick ends.

It is deliciously coloured and textured with lichens.

WHITCHURCH PARISH (52)

Tremaenhir Stones, Crowswood, Solva (SM 826 263) NPRN 305 316

Here at one of the most enigmatic sites in the county the sense of antiquity is almost overpowering. Two homesteads close together shelter under a grove of noisy rook inhabited wytch elms and sycamores. Their farm land stretches out on either side, and the road zig-zags sharply in the centre of the group.

The place name has given cause for speculation in the past. The late John Gibbon was born and lived there for sixty years He informed the Royal Commission surveyor of a tradition in his family that in the days when the farm was a 'sheepwalk' before the enclosures, the sheep were rounded up at the Tri *meini hirion*. He had his initials and the date 1860 cut on one of the standing stones. Perhaps it was he who used another as the simnai fawr (big chimney) lintel in the farmhouse.

Four standing stones can be seen, three of them apparently in line.

The first is anvil-shaped and stands in a field behind Tremaenhir farmhouse. Though small it is of similar shape to others, namely Clegyrn Farm and Trehale, and should not be dismissed casually as a rubbing stone.

The second is a monolith with the date and initials cut on it, and stands beside the road. It is triangular in plan as are other slim members of pairs. The narrow sides taper to a fine wedge-shaped top and the blue stone shows brightly through the lichen where someone has chipped the top and base of this splendid pillar. A young tree is growing against the stone and in summer the undergrowth makes it almost invisible.

Beyond the latter, and through the trees is the third stone.

It does not stand in the middle of the field like many recently erected rubbing stones and should not be dismissed as one.

In the rickyard of Crowswood Farm is a broad blue-stone, the fourth. It will be seen that it is outside the line of the three others, and its position gives weight to the idea that all were once part of a circle or alignment, in the centre of which at a much later date were built the two farm houses, as at Avebury.

There are many large stones in the hedges, or serving as gate posts, all of which may have been once part of the architectural plan.

NEVERN PARISH (53)

Rhos Maen, Newport

(SN 082 398) NPRN 413 140

Two large stones used as gateposts were described by the Royal Commission as being 100 inches and 75 inches high and 96 inches apart, standing in a hedge opposite Tŷ Gwyn Cottages on the Morfa. The cottages have long since disappeared and one of the stones has been removed to widen the gateway. The list published in the *Pembrokeshire Historian* classed the pair as gateposts.

The remaining stone has been included in this collection first because of the belief once held in the locality that the pair of stones were dropped on the present site when being taken to build Trellyffaint cromlech. This relates to legends of stones moving by themselves, or with ease when taken by men to correct places, and the necessity to take certain stones to certain places. Second, the remaining stone is triangular in plan with a sloping chisel-shaped top, both characteristics of the slim members of stone pairs, making it likely that these were indeed a pair. Third, remembering the importance Guy Underwood attached to old gateposts in the landscape plan, the painting may draw attention to the sad loss of many ancient stones. Instead of moving them, perhaps it would be possible to leave the old ones *in situ*, and create new, wider gateways in hedges to accommodate modern farm machinery.

Bibliography

Barber, Chris: *Mysterious Wales.* David & Charles Ltd, Newton Abbot, Devon 1982.

Bord, Janet and Colin: *Mysterious Britain.* Granada Publishing Ltd, London 1982.

Bord, Janet and Colin: *The Secret Country.* Granada Publishing Ltd, London 1982.

Coles, John M: *The God-Dolly from Somerset.* Illustrated London News. November 30th 1968.

Dames, Michael: *The Silbury Treasure.* Thames and Hudson Ltd, London 1976.

Devereux, Paul and Thomson, Ian: *The Ley Hunter's Companion.* Thames and Hudson Ltd, London 1979.

Evans, Henry: *Twr-y-Felin History and Guide to St Davids.* Second Edition, 1923.

Fenton, Richard: *Historical Tour through Pembrokeshire.* 1811.

Graves, Tom: *Dowsing, Techniques and Applications.* Turnstone Books, London 1976.

Graves, Tom: *Needles of Stone.* Granada Publishing Ltd, London 1980.

Grimes, W. F.: *Archaeology, Pembrokeshire National Park.* H.M.S.O. London 1973.

Guest, Lady Charlotte: *Mabinogion.* London 1877.

Havelock Fidler, J.: *Ley Lines.* Turnstone Press Ltd, Wellingborough 1983.

Hill, Ann: *A Visual Encyclopaedia of Unconventional Medicine.* Copplestone Publishing Ltd, London 1978.

Howell, Peter and Beazley, Elisabeth: *The Companion Guide to South Wales.* Collins, London 1977.

Howells, W.: *Cambrian Superstitions.* 1831.

Jones, W. B. and Freeman, E. A.: *The History and Antiquities of St Davids, London and Tenby.* 1856.

Lewis, E. T.: *Llanfyrnach Parish Lore; Mynachlog-Ddu.*

Lewis, J. M.: *The Standing Stones of Pembrokeshire.* The Pembrokeshire Historian 1966, The Pembrokeshire Community Council, Haverfordwest 1966.

Lewis, J. M.: *Excavations at Rhos-y-Clegyrn Prehistoric Site, St Nicholas, Pembrokeshire.* Reprinted from *Archaeologia Cambrensis*: CXXIII 1974.

Macdonnell, Edward: *Archaeology in Australia.* Country Life, April 3rd 1980.

Manby: *The History of the Parish of St Davids.* 1801.

Michell, John: *Megalithomania.* Thames and Hudson, London 1982.

Monmouth, Geoffrey of: *The History of the Kings of Britain.* Penguin Books Ltd, Harmondsworth 1966.

Ormond, John: *Ancient Monuments.* The Oxford Book of Welsh Verse in English, Oxford University Press, Oxford 1983.

Owen, Trefor M.: *Welsh Folk Customs.* National Museum of Wales, Cardiff 1968.

Rees, Vyvyan: *South West Wales, A Shell Guide.* Faber & Faber Ltd, London 1963.

Robins, Dr (Don) G. V.: *Broadcast BBC Radio 4.* 1983

Royal Commission on Ancient Monuments. An Inventory of Ancient Monuments in Wales and Monmouthshire. VII: County Of Pembroke. London 1925.

Radionic Quarterly. The Radionic Association, Banbury.

Screeton, Paul: *Quicksilver Heritage.* Sphere Books Ltd, London 1977.

Thom, A.: *Megalithic Sites in Britain.* The Clarendon Press, Oxford 1967.

Trevelyan, Marie: *Folk Lore and Folk Customs of Wales.* 1909.

Underwood, Guy: *The Pattern of the Past.* Sphere Books Ltd, London 1972.

Watkins, Alfred: *The Old Straight Track.* Sphere Books, London 1974.

Watson, Lyall: *Supernature.* Hodder & Stoughton, London 1974.

Wentz, W. Y. Evans: *The Fairy Faith in Celtic Countries.* Colin Smythe, Gerrards Cross 1977.

Whistler, Laurence: *The English Festivals.* William Heinemann Ltd, London 1947.